ANNA ＿ N ＿ E ＿

THE W ＿ ＿ WAR II YEARS

THE IRISH EMERGENCY

D1610756

Number 28 *of* 1939.

EMERGENCY POWERS ACT, 1939.

AN ACT TO MAKE PROVISION FOR SECURING THE PUBLIC SAFETY AND THE PRESERVATION OF THE STATE IN TIME OF WAR AND, IN PARTICULAR, TO MAKE PROVISION FOR THE MAINTENANCE OF PUBLIC ORDER AND FOR THE PROVISION AND CONTROL OF SUPPLIES AND SERVICES ESSENTIAL TO THE LIFE OF THE COMMUNITY, AND TO PROVIDE FOR DIVERS OTHER MATTERS (INCLUDING THE CHARGING OF FEES ON CERTAIN LICENCES AND OTHER DOCUMENTS) CONNECTED WITH THE MATTERS AFORESAID. [*3rd September,* 1939.]

BE IT ENACTED BY THE OIREACHTAS AS FOLLOWS:—

1.—In this Act—

Definitions.

the word " Minister " means a member of the Government whether he is or is not a Minister having charge of a Department of State;

the word " instrument " means an order, regulation, rule, bye-law, warrant, licence, certificate, or other like document.

2.—(1) The Government may, whenever and so often as they think fit, make by order (in this Act referred to as an emergency order) such provisions as are, in the opinion of the Government, necessary or expedient for securing the public safety or the preservation of the State, or for the maintenance of public order, or for the provision and control of supplies and services essential to the life of the community.

Emergency orders.

(2) Without prejudice to the generality of the foregoing subsection of this section, the Government may do by an emergency order all or any of the following things, that is to say:—

The World War II Years
The Irish Emergency

An Illustrated History

Helen Litton

Picture Research:
Peter Costello

WOLFHOUND PRESS

Published in 2001 by
Wolfhound Press Ltd
68 Mountjoy Square
Dublin 1, Ireland
Tel: (353-1) 874 0354
Fax: (353-1) 872 0207

© 2001 Helen Litton

British Library Cataloguing in Publication Data
A catalogue record for this book is available from the British Library.

Uncredited pictures are from private sources or of unknown copyright. The
publishers have made every reasonable effort to contact the copyright
holders of material reproduced in this book. If any involuntary infringement
of copyright has occurred, sincere apologies are offered and the owners of
such copyright are requested to contact the publishers.

ISBN 0-86327-859-0

10 9 8 7 6 5 4 3 2 1

Opposite page (top): *ESB advertisement*

Cover Design: Slick Fish Design
Typesetting and book design: Wolfhound Press
Printed in Spain by GraphyCems

Contents

Irish neutrality, on which she placed a generous interpretation, permitted the Germans to maintain in Dublin an espionage-centre, a window into Britain, which operated throughout the war and did incalculable harm to the Allied cause. But from the naval point of view there was an even more deadly factor: this was the loss of the naval bases in southern and western Ireland, which had been available to the Royal Navy during the first world war but were now forbidden them. To compute how many men and how many ships this denial was costing, month after month, was hardly possible; but the total was substantial and tragic. From these bases escorts could have sailed further out into the Atlantic, and provided additional cover for the hard-pressed convoys: from these bases, destroyers and corvettes could have been refuelled quickly, and tugs sent out to ships in distress: from these bases, the Battle of the Atlantic might have been fought on something like equal terms. As it was, the bases were denied: escorts had to go 'the long way round' to get to the battlefield, and return to harbour at least two days earlier than would have been necessary: the cost, in men and ships, added months to the struggle, and ran up a score which Irish eyes a-smiling on the day of Allied victory were not going to cancel.

NICHOLAS MONSARRAT, *THE CRUEL SEA*, 1951

Opposite page (top): Call to arms.

Foreword

T he quote opposite, from Nicholas Monsarrat, leaps off the page today, fifty years after it was written. It expresses not only outrage, at unnecessary and wasteful loss, but also a depth of cold contempt that can still bring a chill, particularly to an Irish reader.

I belong to the baby-boom generation, born just after the end of the Second World War. I found it difficult to comprehend why my country, one renowned as brave in battle and indomitable in defeat, steered clear of involvement in this conflict. Why was it not obvious how evil the Third Reich was, and that if it won, all civilisation would lose? Were the crimes of the British in general, and the more recent brutalities of the War of Independence, enough to absolve us of the moral responsibility to join in the great battle of that generation, however little help we could offer? But the reality was far more complex, and perspectives at the time were quite different.

There are many ways to write about Ireland during the 'Emergency', from the humour of Patrick Campbell's risible experiences in the Naval Reserve and Bertie Smyllie's long-running battle with the censorship authorities, to the more serious and considered studies that have emerged recently, detailing the real costs and benefits of the policy of neutrality in both the short and the long term. You can conjure up anecdotes about thrice-used ounces of tea, cross-border smuggling, and the fear of the 'glimmer man', and leaven them with selected cartoons from *Dublin Opinion* (which spoke for the rest of the country also, one assumes). But the really important question has to remain unanswered, because it never can be answered satisfactorily — was this Ireland's finest hour?

This survey of Ireland during the Second World War is necessarily short, and within it I could deal only briefly with a wide range of topics. However, I hope it will serve as a factual picture of a new nation facing its first great test, and a society which, although often seen negatively as closed and inward-looking, was beginning to respond to twentieth-century changes and currents of thought.

Once again, I have to thank Wolfhound Press for giving me the opportunity to write this book, the sixth in the series of *Illustrated Histories*. I am deeply grateful to Peter Costello, not only for his excellent picture research, but also for several important resources which he indicated to me. I would like to dedicate this book to my parents, Phyllis Brolly and John Daly O'Sullivan, who are of the generation which reached adulthood during the 'Emergency' period, and helped to build the Ireland that developed after it.

Left: The Gate Theatre combined an enthusiasm for Gaelic with the presentation of advanced modern plays from abroad.

Introduction

The Second World War (1939–1945) was rooted in the refusal by Germany, under its Chancellor Adolf Hitler, to accept the limitations imposed on the country by the Treaty of Versailles, agreed at the end of the First World War. Hitler's ruling National Socialist party (Nazis) preached the doctrine of an Aryan 'master race', which would overcome all lesser races and extend its power as far as possible across the globe. Driven by this doctrine, Germany began to threaten its neighbours — firstly Austria, which it occupied in March 1938.

Powerful European countries such as Britain and France had mutual treaty obligations for defence. However, the smaller countries of the continent were outside this network, and as a result Hitler's early aggressions were largely ignored. However, when he invaded Czechoslovakia in March 1939, Britain and France declared that a similar invasion of Poland by the Germans would not be tolerated. On 1 September 1939, Hitler, having allied with Russia, invaded Poland and consequently, Britain and France declared war on Germany.

Left: The gentle pastoral image of Ireland encouraged by both the government of de Valera and the tourist trade. Courtesy ITA

After a quiescent period of about six months, known as the 'Phoney War', Germany invaded Norway, Denmark, Holland and Belgium, all of which had declared themselves neutral, and full-scale war broke out in earnest. Unlike the First World War, this war was a modern one, waged as fiercely in the sea and in the air as on land. Air raids targeted cities packed with civilians, and German U-boats (submarines) targeted all traffic across the Atlantic, threatening Britain's supply lines.

When Germany attacked Britain, it was driven back by naval and air forces in the Battle of Britain (August–September 1940). Hitler then invaded Greece and Yugoslavia in April 1941. Italy's fascist rule, under Benito Mussolini and allied with Hitler, was defeated by the Allies and forced to make peace in September 1943. Germany broke her alliance with Russia and invaded that country in June 1941, but was defeated by Russian forces and by appalling winters, and was ultimately forced to retreat in 1944, greatly weakened. Finally, in June 1944, the Allies masterminded a massive invasion of Europe through Normandy, and liberated France. They pressed eastwards through Germany and, in April

Previous page (top): German Chancellor and Nazi leader, Adolf Hitler.

1945, they reached Berlin which had already been attacked by Russian troops. The Soviets had beaten the German forces westwards to their capital city through Poland. Germany surrendered in early May 1945.

On another front, in the Far East, Japan had attacked US forces at Pearl Harbour in December 1941, forcing America into the War. This conflict finally ended when America dropped the first atomic bombs ever used in aggression, on the cities of Hiroshima and Nagasaki, in August 1945. These bombs killed 225,000 people, and the devastation they created resulted in Japan's surrender.

Casualty figures for the Second World War were enormous — about 28 million people over the six years, including large numbers of civilians. One of the most chilling casualty-lists is that of European Jews, about six million of whom were deliberately exterminated in concentration camps as a result of Nazi racial theories, in what became known as the Holocaust.

Right: *The retreat from Dunkirk, as recorded by an official British war artist.*

An cóiscrío
an tsín
mo
ċar lear
tír fó cuinn
mo
mo 1
2
3
mo
an muir astruaṡ
toraiġ
arainn
an blascaod
corca dorċa
P. de B.
o slig jail
na daoine uaisle
cark
an cóiscrío

- Aḋarca fada ar buaiḃ.
- The sea-divided Gael.
× - Poteen deposits.
⌂ - Cnuic ġlasa.
① - Nrú lárc.
② - Boston.
③ - Springfield Mass.
mo - Money Order Office.
G.B.S. - Seoirse Drian Seoirge.
······ - Pratie Hokers' Routes.

Left: The Gaelic world view satirised by Myles na gCopaleen and drawn by Sean O'Sullivan for the jacket of An Béal Bocht. *America meant money orders, from Irish exiles.*

At the beginning of the War, countries declaring neutrality included Sweden, Switzerland, Portugal and the United States. Ireland also declared its neutrality, but it was much harder for the British and their allies to accept this decision. Ireland had been part of the British Empire for so long, and in 1939 was still part of the Commonwealth — how could it stand aloof? But in Ireland the view was rather different, and the majority of the population, whether or not they might be nursing bitter memories of British rule, felt that there was no point in being dragged into such a large conflict, in which a small country could have little influence or sufficient ability to defend itself.

Independent Policy

When the Irish Free State was established in 1922, after the signing of the Anglo-Irish Treaty, the new government felt that it was important to consolidate its new-found independence from Britain, particularly with regard to foreign policy. For example, the Free State sent a diplomatic representative of its own to the League of Nations in 1923.

When Eamon de Valera and his Fianna Fáil party came to power in 1932, they began to decouple some of the links that still remained between Ireland and Britain. A bill was passed abolishing the oath of allegiance to the monarchy which TDs took on entering the Dáil, and the office of British governor-general was downgraded. However, de Valera did not want to antagonise Britain unnecessarily by employing more aggressive actions. This was partly because of the vulnerable position of thousands of Irish emigrants in that country and partly, perhaps, to keep lines open to the Unionists in Northern Ireland, in the hope of eventually achieving Irish unity. Equally, the British did not want to look as if they were trying to push Ireland out of the Commonwealth, which would have been greatly resented by dominions such as Canada.

Above: *The Irish Treaty ports and the other great naval bases of northern Europe, which were critical to the war.*

De Valera embarked on one course of action, however, that met with a strong reaction from the British; he decided to refuse the payment of land annuities that were due under the terms of the Anglo-Irish Treaty. (This land settlement had been part of the Treaty agreement, but had been kept secret, and never ratified by Dáil Éireann.) In retaliation, the British government imposed a 20 per cent duty on two-thirds of Irish exports to Britain (Ireland's largest market at the time). The subsequent 'economic war', of high tariffs and restricted exports, cost both countries a great deal, but naturally hit harder in Ireland, which was very dependent on its export trade. Fianna Fáil introduced a protectionist policy, hoping to achieve as much economic self-sufficiency as possible. De Valera was making the point that political freedom required economic freedom too. His 1937 Constitution copperfastened the Free State's 'inalienable, indefeasible, and sovereign' rights, without any mention of the Commonwealth or the British monarchy.

The economic war ended in 1938 with the signing of an Anglo-Irish agreement. The Irish were to make a once-off payment of £10 million to Britain in return for which its land annuities claim would be dropped. Another part of the agreement related to defence and focused on the status of the three 'Treaty ports', Berehaven, Cobh and Lough Swilly, all of which were in the Free State. These ports were considered to be important for Britain's strategic interests, and had remained under British control after the ratification of the Anglo-Irish Treaty. Now, in 1938, they were finally handed over to Irish control, much to the dismay of politicians such as Winston Churchill, who were aware of the importance they might well have in the near future.

However, de Valera promised that the ports would not be used by anyone against Britain's interests, and he had said already that mutual self-interest would make Britain and Ireland the closest possible allies if either of them was threatened. He attended the League of Nations Assembly in 1938 as its President, just as Hitler was threatening Czechoslovakia. There he expressed his hopes for a peaceful settlement, and sent a note of support to Neville Chamberlain, prime minister of Great Britain and Northern Ireland. But it was clear that Europe was being increasingly dominated by the great powers, and that the League of Nations was not strong enough to prevent the plunge into warfare that Europe, and much of the world, was about to take. Ireland was to find itself isolated and left to make its own path through a tangled web of relationships.

Opposite page (top): Dublin city centre.
Photo: G.A. Duncan

1: Government Action

Britain and France both declared war on Germany on 3 September 1939. On the same day, the Irish Free State passed an Emergency Powers Act, which would remain in force until 2 September 1946. Europe was at war: Ireland was on Emergency Status.

At this time the Fianna Fáil party was in power, and the government was headed by Eamon de Valera, who was Taoiseach and also Minister for External Affairs. Frank Aiken was Minister for Defence and Sean Lemass — one of the most energetic of de Valera's ministers — was made Minister of the Department of Supplies. This was a new department, and its creation was an acknowledgement of the fact that matters of supply were going to become of crucial importance. Sean MacEntee was made Minister for Industry and Commerce in place of Sean Lemass, and Sean T. O'Kelly became Minister for Finance.

The opposition parties expressed their support for government policy on neutrality, although Fine Gael had reservations about opposing any British incursion. From time to time, calls were made in the Dáil for for a national coalition to be formed, but the most the government offered the opposition was a Defence Committee, with representatives from all parties. This was basically a talking-shop, with no powers of its own. Dáil debates became limited to matters of domestic interest only, as international affairs could not be discussed.

Supplies

The question of supplies turned out to be even more important than expected. Initially, there had been a vague sense that the Second World War would be fought on mainland Europe, as the First World War had been. No one expected the submarine war-fare that turned islands like Britain and Ireland into beleaguered outposts cut off from their normal trade-routes. As an Irish naval officer remarked, 'realisation dawned in Ireland that the country was surrounded by water and that the sea was of vital impor-tance to her'.

The threat to supplies led to an intense effort to produce as much food and as many products as possible within the state, and also to exploit whatever natural resources could be found. At the same time, as much raw material as possible had to be kept from leaving the country. The Emergency Powers Act gave the state the necessary authority to prevent exports of essential commodities and also to impose controls over imports, in order to use foreign-exchange supplies as carefully as possible. The Act was a dictatorial piece of legislation, giving the government stringent powers over all aspects of administration.

Lemass was optimistic that Ireland could remain self-sufficient for some time, as many raw materials were available in the country. However, prospects of self-sufficiency were limited. Ireland was utterly dependent on outside suppliers for commodi-ties such as pig-iron and pig-lead, asbestos, copper and electrical equipment, as well as large supplies of timber, wheat, maize and petroleum. When the War began, the sole supplier of coal to Ireland was Britain — it also owned 64 per cent of the shipping

Above: 'Glory be! The Glimmer Man!'
The terror of government regulation in a middle-class home, complete with maid, a famous Dublin Opinion *cartoon.*

Below: In rural areas hand-won turf was the main fuel resource in wartime. Many city people also had bog allotments in the Dublin and Wicklow mountains.

I should like to see this small, weak country of Ireland demonstrate, as it has never been demonstrated in the history of the world before, that it is not by bread alone that man must live and that, whatever may have been the material squabbles that precipitated war in the world, to us the only issue of significance is whether Christianity shall survive.... I am convinced that, were we to accept that charge and face that duty, posterity would have it to tell that in the darkest hour of crisis, when danger seemed heaviest and perils greatest, Ireland, recognising her destiny, faced it without counting the material cost and that, whatever her losses were, the undying glory of having stood as a nation for great principles and in defence of the higher freedom had secured for her and her people immortality in human history.

JAMES DILLON, 17 JULY 1941

Above: *The night mail carrying urgent news past the community kitchen in Pearse Street. This produced 2,000 take-away dinners a day for the poor of Dublin in 1941.* Photo: G.A. Duncan.

Right: For most young people in rural areas the lack of supplies which Sean Lemass struggled with as minister meant merely fewer sweets and cigarettes.

which normally entered Irish ports. As the war went on, Britain became increasingly unwilling to use much of its scarce resources to keep Ireland supplied with essentials.

To alleviate the situation, a system of compulsory tillage was established, which greatly increased the acreage of the country under wheat, but which was resented by many farmers. A drive to grow more potatoes was also begun. For a time, Ireland still had surplus capacity in rubber and cement and Lemass bargained these with Britain for other raw materials. These were shipped to Ireland in strictest secrecy, and finished goods were sent back. Finally, in March 1941, Irish Shipping was established, with three ships, to try to keep supplies reaching the Free State; by the end of the war it was carrying one million tons of cargo into the country, two-thirds of which was wheat. Butter, eggs and meat remained plentiful in the Free State, but tea was in short supply and an active black market developed around it. Britain needed Irish exports of cattle, although these had to stop during 1941, when the Free State suffered an outbreak of foot-and-mouth disease.

In late 1941, Churchill tried to use the question of supplies to force Ireland to modify her neutrality. In 1940, Ireland had chartered ships through the British, and it was now proposed that this facility be ended. If this happened, the Free State would be forced to survive on its own meagre shipping resources. Greece and Norway were to be warned to charter ships only to Allied countries. The plan was not carried through, but petrol supplies to Ireland were cut by half. The public realised this only when petrol pumps ran dry over Christmas, and people found themselves unable to get home from family visits. In early 1943, the Free State threatened to stop exports of Guinness if it could not get enough wheat — at that time, 80 per cent of beer supplies in Northern Ireland came from the Free State. Britain responded with an offer of 20,000 tons of wheat.

Lemass wanted increased spending on housing, in order to create employment as well as homes, but even by early 1940 supplies of building materials were dwindling. The manufacture of concrete and brick stopped; there was no fuel for cement-mixers, nor copper for hot water-pipes; steel instead of wood was used for windows, and some lead piping was also used. By 1943, building costs had risen by up to 43 per cent.

Spending on roads also dropped. By 1941, there was no longer any petrol available for private cars, and the money brought in by road taxes dropped accordingly. Cars were put up on blocks for the duration. The Road Traffic Acts were amended, increasing the numbers permitted to be carried in buses, and coming down harder on bicycle theft; a bicycle pump was worth its weight in gold. To save wear and tear on tyres, vehicle speed limits were reduced. Public transport in Dublin ceased after 9 p.m.

De Valera and Lemass were worried about high levels of unemployment. This was more an urban than a rural problem, as factories began to run out of raw materials and closed down. The Unemployment (Relief Works) Bill of 1940 envisaged huge road-building projects, such as two inner ring-roads in Dublin, but shortage of supplies stopped the plans from moving further. The Department of Local Government was given powers to begin relief works in any area — local authorities were reluctant to begin such schemes themselves, since they were already short of money for basic services. However, contractors building local authority houses insisted on finding their own workforces, and could not be forced to use people on unemployment assistance instead. Because the bulk of unemployment was in Dublin, it was planned to remove many unemployed men to the country, to live in labour camps and work on the land, or the bogs, cutting turf for fuel. The first experiment in this way, at Clonsast bog in County Offaly, was poorly organised, and most of the displaced urban-dwellers absconded; later camps proved more successful.

The Department of Finance established an Economy Committee, but there was always a huge gap between the economies that the Department decided were necessary, and the amount of political support the government was willing to risk losing. One of the long-term results of the Emergency was a policy of state intervention in major areas of the economy. An interdepartmental committee on Emergency Measures laid plans for alleviating distress if there was an invasion, or if the country became completely cut off.

Defence

In the early stages of the war, the question of the Treaty ports loomed large, and there was a cabinet Defence Committee to consider measures to be taken if the ports were captured by force. De Valera did not put defence expenditure at the top of his priorities, because neutrality ought to imply a lack of necessity for high levels of such expenditure. A limited defence scheme had been prepared, but even this was pared down in the early stages of the conflict. By the end of the War, only 20 per cent of public expenditure was devoted to defence, a small percentage at such a time.

Invasion was a real fear, whether by Britain to take the ports back, or by Germany seeking a back door into Britain. Accordingly, in late 1940, a plan was drawn up which was to be implemented in the event of invasion. It divided the state into eight regions, each with County Commissioners and a Regional Commissioner, to run the administration if the government

WORK IN PROGRESS !

THERE is work to do ! Big work—the re-building of a Nation. Good work—the defences that guard our peace. Interesting work—the Ireland of to-morrow taking shape. And there will be talk to-morrow of those who do this work to-day if it is well done.

HELP US TO MAKE A GREAT JOB OF IT !

CONDITIONS OF ENTRY: Age 18 to 25 years, good character, unemployed, without dependants. When you have completed your first twelve months you will be a free agent as to whether you wish to continue, to join the Regular Army, or to return home.

CONDITIONS OF SERVICE

1/- a day plus a lump sum of £10 on discharge after 12 months' service. Good Conduct Badges may be issued after a month's service. You will get 3d. a day extra for this. If appointed a squad leader you will get 6d. a day more. For clerks, storemen, tailors, shoemakers, cooks, additional pay is given. Food, uniform, and holidays as for Regular Army.

JOIN THE

CONSTRUCTION CORPS

COLLINS' BARRACKS, DUBLIN

Recruiting is confined to the Dublin area for the present

should fall. They would have powers to requisition livestock and essential supplies, and to fix prices. If these commissioners could not function, the Garda Síochána would take over control. Public servants were instructed that if the country were invaded, they should carry out their basic duties as usual, but were not to give any cooperation of military value to the invader.

An Air Raid Precautions Act was passed in 1939, and plans were also made to evacuate children from cities in case of bombing raids — up to 70,000 individuals from Dublin alone. As the early stages of the War went badly for the Allied forces, plans were prepared for up to 160,000 people to leave Dublin for rural areas. Food shortages raised the prospect of communal feeding centres, but by 1942 it was decided that such drastic innovations would not be necessary. As the secretary of the Department of Local Government said, there were 'strong moral and social reasons for not interfering in normal family life', even by providing meals for schoolchildren as the Irish Housewives' Association had suggested.

Opposite page:
Organised work in
a free democracy.

Right: 'Work' in
fascist Germany
meant slavery –
the notorious
legend over the
gates of
Auschwitz.

2: Neutrality

For the Irish Free State, the choice of neutrality was an important aspect of independence. All political parties were agreed on it, and the only dissenting voice in the Dáil was that of James Dillon, of Fine Gael, who felt that Ireland was failing in its international responsibility by staying out of the war:

> ... it is a constant source of shame to me that our people who have so long been the champions of liberty in the world should now be represented before the world as knowing no difference between Germany ... and the Commonwealth of Nations and the USA....

Others may have silently agreed with him but decided, pragmatically, that the risks of entering the war were far greater than anything the entry of a small country could achieve. When de Valera broadcast to the nation, he said:

> We resolved that the aim of our policy would be to keep our people out of a war. I said in the Dáil that with our history, with our experience of the last war, and with part of our country still unjustly severed from us, we felt that no other decision and no other policy was possible.

An immediate effect of the government's decision on neutrality was a huge influx of people from Britain. These included returning emigrants as well as Britons who were seeking to avoid the War ('flyboys'). For several weeks Irish ports were jammed with ferries. For Britain, the most important immediate result of Ireland's neutrality was the loss of the 'Treaty ports'. Winston Churchill, in particular, was frustrated enough to consider taking back the ports by force, whatever the consequences. However, a report by Lord Cranborne pointed out that:

> We have forces in Northern Ireland. We can strengthen them and invade Éire. That, if the worst comes to the worst, is what we shall be obliged to do. But ... it will be very expensive; it will not be very edifying; and it will arouse a considerable opposition among Irish elements in the United States and even in the Dominions; above all, it will rally the whole Irish nation behind Mr de Valera, which is the last thing we want to do.

Above: *British cartoon by Illingworth presenting the British view of neutrality in the context of an enslaved Europe.*

Opposite page (top): *The Irish navy on watch.*

> ...*when any German activity developed we were promptly informed
> and all relevant material was handed over to us. Gradually, a certain
> geographical interpretation of neutrality was developed. We procured
> the non-internment of our RAF personnel. That was a stiff one, but
> we got over it. Assistance from the Éire Government included rigid
> surveillance of the German legation, the impounding of their wireless
> transmitter and close understanding with the British intelligence serv-
> ice. In this underground of espionage and intrigue a British authority
> could never achieve what was achieved by a native authority.*
>
> SIR JOHN MAFFEY, ANNUAL REPORT 1945/6

Invasion of Ireland was a popular subject in the British press. In November 1940, for example, an article in *The Economist* said:

If the ports become a matter of life and death — for Ireland as well as England — there can be only one way out: we must take them. That would of course revive all the old bitterness. But if bitterness there must be, let us have the bitterness and the bases, not the bitterness alone....

Above: James Dillon, stylish opposition member and outspoken critic of neutrality.

In the early stages of the war, the ports would have been of use in helping to defend the convoys of Allied ships which crossed the Atlantic. However, as the war shifted eastwards, the convoys soon began to concentrate on the northern route, past Scotland and Northern Ireland. Thus the ports in the Free State became of far less significance to the Allies. Besides, a 1936 British Army assessment had estimated that it would cost £276,000 to defend the ports, and that 14,000 soldiers would be needed in each. Defending them in a hostile Ireland would be impracticable.

International Relations

Because the Free State was neutral, it maintained diplomatic contacts with all the belligerent countries. Members of the diplomatic corps in Dublin included Sir John Maffey, UK Representative in Éire; John Cudahy and later David Gray, US legates; Dr Edouard Hempel, representing Germany; Vincenzo Berardis of Italy; and Satsuya Beppu of Japan. The Free State was accused of allowing the Axis powers (Germany, Italy and Japan) to spy on Allied activity, but in fact very little successful espionage took place. The Irish Army's intelligence arm, G2, together with the Garda Síochána (police force) security branch, G3, were quite efficient in forestalling any efforts in that direction. They were staffed by intelligence officers who, having come through the War of Independence and the Civil War, had developed much valuable expertise in espionage.

Around the month of December 1940, Germany's Foreign Minister, Ribbentrop, attempted to send intelligence officers into the German legation in Ireland. However, de Valera insisted that they would be arrested as soon as they arrived in the country. Subsequently, in January 1941, German bombs fell in several parts of Ireland — this may or may not have been a coincidence.

On the British side, the loss of defence rights in Ireland in 1938 had meant a consequent loss of intelligence-gathering capacity. British intelligence agencies such as MI5 and the Supplementary Intelligence Service (SIS) did their best to make up the shortfall. They also maintained contacts with the Northern Ireland's Royal Ulster Constabulary (RUC) who were not, however, well informed about Free State security matters. In fact, the Irish had made an approach to the British about intelligence liaison in 1938. In addition Joseph Walshe, secretary to the Department of External Affairs, had contacted

Above: Eamon de Valera, architect of Irish neutrality.
Photo:
G. A. Duncan

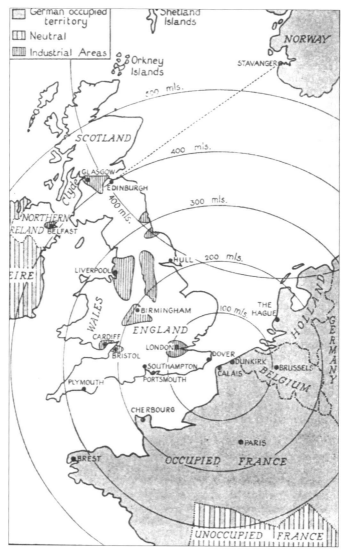

Above: *Ireland north and south was well within the flying range of German bombers, as Belfast, Dublin and other places learnt to their cost.*

the Dominions Office with information about a Nazi group operating in Dublin. Such links were maintained throughout the War. The British seem to have felt that the officials concerned were working without the knowledge or permission of the Irish government, but de Valera was fully aware of these contacts, and encouraged them in private.

It has become clear over the last number of years, as records of the period are released and memoirs published, that Ireland was distinctly 'neutral for the British'. De Valera cooperated far more with the Allies than most people in Ireland (or indeed Britain) had previously realised. During the Blitz, he offered refuge to British women and children, and he protested publicly about Germany's invasions of Holland and Belgium in May 1940, despite Hempel's complaints. Irish coastwatchers deliberately broadcast information on shipping movements (including submarines) to their regional commands, which radioed them on to Dublin; Britain could then pick them up from there.

The exchange of information benefited both countries, and reassured Britain that, for example, the legations of Axis powers in Dublin were being closely watched. Of course, the activities of

[Russia and America] were no voluntary crusaders leaping into the arena in unreflecting and disinterested enthusiasm for high moral principle. They had made no move when others were wantonly attacked. They remained neutral when Denmark and Norway, Holland and Belgium, Jugoslavia and Greece were, in turn, ravaged and enslaved. They fought because they had to, because they had no choice left, because they were attacked, because being attacked, they needs must fight or submit to a conqueror's yoke. And little Ireland was not attacked. That is the difference. That is the sole difference. For there is nothing more certain than that Ireland also would have fought back if she had been attacked.

CAPTAIN HENRY HARRISON (EX-BRITISH ARMY) RESPONDING TO AN ARTICLE
ON IRISH NEUTRALITY IN *NEW YORK TIMES,* 1943

Above:
David Gray,
United States
Ambassador.

Above:
Sir John
Maffey, British
representative
in Dublin.

Above:
T. J. Kiernan,
Ireland's man
in Berlin.

British and American intelligence-gatherers were also being closely watched. G2 had someone inside the SIS branch in Dublin, and was able to monitor it completely until the end of the War. No complaint was made to Britain about the existence of such an organisation within a neutral country, because a new branch would simply be set up instead, and might be harder to infiltrate.

The director of the National Library in Dublin, Dr Richard Hayes, was a skilled cryptographer, and managed to break the German codes while studying messages from the German legation in Dublin; the British Government Code and Cipher School had not done so. This information was also shared. The British Air Ministry was allowed the use of an air corridor over County Donegal, west of Lough Erne, and also the use of the seaplane base at Foynes, near Shannon, for civil aviation needs. When the police discovered plans for a German/IRA attack on Northern Ireland, they immediately passed the details on to MI5.

Allied complaints were made to the Irish government about the existence of a radio transmitter in the German legation, through which Hempel sent weather reports. Much later in the war, as preparations mounted in 1944 for the invasion of Normandy, pressure on this issue became intense, and Hempel was warned that the transmitter would have to be closed down as a danger to neutrality. The radio set was lodged in a bank — the German legation having one key to it and the Irish government the other.

America, though initially neutral itself, was annoyed by Ireland's neutrality and tried to put pressure on de Valera. Following a visit to the United States by Michael Costello of the Irish Army, America provided the Free State with 20,000 rifles, to aid in self-defence in case of German invasion — probably an attempt to influence Ireland away from neutrality. However, neither Britain nor the US was prepared to provide the extent of weaponry which could help the Free State to defend the 'Treaty ports' against capture by Allied forces. Hempel had given de Valera a guarantee that Germany would not invade Ireland, but Sir John Maffey was not able to give the same categorical assurance in relation to Britain. The German view was that invasion of Ireland would actually be very difficult: Wales and Cornwall blocked the direct route over the Irish Sea, and the British fleet was strong.

David Gray, the US representative in Ireland after March 1940, was deeply opposed to Ireland's neutrality policy, and refused to see any merit in it at all. He was close to President Roosevelt, and his reports had great influence in Washington. In late 1943, after the USA had entered the war, he argued that the States should demand air and port facilities in Ireland and also insist that all Axis diplomats be removed from the country.

Above: *Vincenzo Berardis, Italian Ambassador in Dublin.*

Above: *Satsuya Beppu, the Japanese Consul in Dublin.*

Above: *Dr Edouard Hempel, the German Ambassador.*

All photos: Adolf Morath

He used a threat to cut off supplies of raw materials to Ireland as a back-up to his demands. However, there was no real military purpose behind these demands — no convoys passed the south of England now, so the ports no longer mattered — and the main point was to get de Valera to refuse, in writing, the use of the ports, so that Ireland would lose any US sympathy after the end of the war and be punished for her neutrality.

A note was sent to the British cabinet seeking support for the US demands, but only two members of the cabinet were really in sympathy with it. However, American and British Notes were presented to the Irish government in February 1944, and de Valera was extremely annoyed at what he saw as an infringement of sovereignty. He replied coldly, pointing out Ireland's espionage successes, and the fact that no foreign legation in the country was allowed to carry out intelligence activities. Both the Notes and the reply were leaked. There was a huge wave of public support for the government, and Gray had to be given a police escort for a short time.

Above: *Cartoon for an American journal attacking the supposed 'U-boat dens' in Éire (the sign in the background is headed 'Neutral Éire').* The Nation (New York)

*The German internees at the Curragh have blended themselves so inti-
mately into the life of Newbridge — the nearest town to their camp —
that nobody now turns his head as a German sailor or airman goes
by. They are free to walk about as they will.*

*…These men, almost without exception, are now so poor that they
will do any odd job around the town to earn a few pence. Since the col-
lapse of Germany no money has come to them at all. About eighty of
them work regularly on the bog, cutting turf side by side with the local
turf-cutters. Another fifty work on the neighbouring farms, cutting
hedges and so on. A few of them have found work where their technical education is of advantage. One man has been converting old
motor-cars so that they can be used as tractors for ploughs.*

*…And how do the people of Newbridge feel about these two hun-
dred and fifty Germans who have come among them? They are agreed
that the German is an amazing worker. One man said: 'I saw one of
them ploughing in a hailstorm. He took off his coat and rolled up his
sleeves. I'm tough enough, but I wouldn't do it.'*

PATRICK CAMPBELL, AN IRISHMAN'S DIARY, 24 MAY 1945

*…I thought of my friends in Dublin, their kindness and intelligence,
their attitude of mingled curiosity and pity, together with a kind of
uneasiness about their neutrality, like the uneasiness behind the land-
scape, behind the Liffey at sunset, or the street-markets lit up in the
rainy evenings. Are the wisest people in the world those who have kept
their calendar at 1938? Has everyone else gone mad? Who are right,
those who cling obstinately to peace, their hard-won convalescence, or
we who feel that, until we know what we are prepared to die for, we are
not fully alive?*

CYRIL CONNOLLY, 'COMMENT'
HORIZON VOL V, NO 25, JANUARY 1942

Above: The Mail Boat arrives at 'Dunleary' (as it was then often spelt) — the essential link between Britain and Ireland for workers, tourists and secret agents.

By late 1942, unofficial policy allowed captured British airmen to go home. However, captured Germans were interned. The reason given was that only those forced to land during operational flights, not training flights, would be interned. Of course, any German aircraft flying near Ireland were operational, and their occupants couldn't claim to be on training flights, as the British could and did. The German legate protested vigorously at this distinction, but without success. Of 142 Allied planes which landed on Irish soil, 47 were refuelled and departed and 27 were salvaged and sent up to Northern Ireland; only 45 pilots were interned. On the other hand, all 55 Germans who landed were interned. Any information about the German planes was passed on to Britain. Allied seamen were also allowed to leave, but the Curragh internment camp held 214 captured German sailors. Any German spies uncovered were imprisoned, but the one British spy who was found was let go.

Opposite page: The aftermath of the bombs on the North Strand — a deliberate act of revenge for Éire's aid to Belfast?

*I think when the success of the [German] invasion had been assured,
it would have emerged that the respectable Xs, the Anglo-Irish
Herrenvolk of Ulster and the Dublin suburbs, would prove the more
satisfactory accomplices in establishing the German hegemony...There
would have been a dazzling display of 'correctness'...divine service
with prayers for the King and the British Empire would continue to be
permitted in the Protestant churches. Certainly the inevitable bias of
German correctness would have been towards the Anglo-Saxon,
towards bridge and fox-hunting, and away from the Irish, from
ceilidhes and hurley matches and language festivals. A master race
will be at times indulgent to these regional enthusiasms but will not
participate in them...There had been in Ireland eminent German
Celtic scholars who had not managed to conceal their contempt for the
modern representatives of those Celtic peoples whose early history
enthralled them. Nazi philosophy was permeated with race snobbery
and we are outwardly a rustic and unpretentious people...In the Nazi
hierarchy of races the Irish would not I think have ranked high.*

HUBERT BUTLER, 'THE INVADER WORE SLIPPERS' [1950]

FROM *ESCAPE FROM THE ANTHILL*, 1985

Left: *Wartime wedding between a British internee at the Curragh and a local girl he met on parole.*
Photo: *Irish Independent*

There were many crash-landings in Ireland, of both British and German planes. Dead British airmen were brought to the border and handed over to the British Army, though in some cases they were buried in Ireland by family request. Most German casualties are buried in the German Military Cemetery at Glencree, County Wicklow where they were gathered together in 1959. Around the coasts, bodies were washed up from ships, submarines and crashed planes, and usually buried near where they were found.

Views on Neutrality

The morality of Ireland's choice of neutrality has always caused intense argument, both at the time of the War and during the years since. Many commentators have felt that the country had little choice in the matter; small and poorly-defended, it would have been overwhelmed, and there was little point in dragging the population into a maelstrom. It has been argued that Ireland was more useful to the Allies in staying aloof, as otherwise Germany would undoubtedly have invaded it and become a greater threat to Britain. It was also argued that by allowing many thousands to fight in the British defence forces, the Free

State was almost as good as a belligerent itself. The Free State seemed to end up with the name of neutrality, with all the criticism and contempt that that attracted, while suffering many of the disadvantages of war.

De Valera emphasised the rights of small nations to make this kind of decision themselves, and reminded the country that it had taken a long time to get rid of the last invader, without inviting new (or old) masters in again. Frank Aiken defended neutrality equally vigorously in a memorandum sent to members of the government, saying that:

> [it] ... has in fact always been one of the difficult problems in human relationships. Instead of earning the respect and goodwill of both belligerents it is regarded by both with hatred and contempt.... In the modern total warfare it is not a condition of peace with both belligerents, but rather a condition of limited warfare with both....

The War itself was not seen by many in Ireland as a moral matter, a need to defend civilisation — just something which Ireland did well to keep out of. Indeed, the motives of the Allies were later impugned by historians claiming that no one had 'moral' motives for fighting the war, merely motives of strategy and power balance. Perhaps it would have been better to leave Hitler alone and try to change Germany from within. Anyway, the War had led to the rise of Stalin and the establishment of Communism all over eastern Europe — was this a good result? There is little doubt today, however, that Nazism had to be fought, for the sake of democracy and human rights, and that Ireland benefited as much as anyone else from the results of this fight. There probably would have been some kind of split in the country if neutrality had been abandoned, but it seems likely that Irish people would have been two-thirds in favour of the Allied cause.

Another important factor in the neutrality argument was the question of partition. Ireland's neutrality was regarded with intense bitterness in Northern Ireland, and it drove the two parts of the island further apart. If Ireland had been a participant, relations might have warmed to some extent, leading to greater rapprochement after the war. Churchill, driven by desperation, twice offered to facilitate the creation of a united Ireland if the Free State joined the war, but the Unionists would never have accepted this for a moment, and de Valera was well aware of that. Naturally, Stormont was appalled by such treachery, and was confirmed in its suspicions of British commitment to Northern Ireland.

"ALWAYS AT YOUR SERVICE"

"What a happy thought this was for an imbromptu dinner party"

Table D'Hote Lunch, 2/3
Delicious Composite Teas,
1/-, 1/6, 1/9, 2/- and 2/6

Theatre Dinner Served
at 4/- from 6 p.m.

Suppers 1/9, 2'-, 2/6, 2/9. Served till 11 p.m.
Club Dinners specially catered for

METROPOLE *Restaurant*

Above: Eating out in wartime Dublin could be a lavish affair, as many visitors found.

Above: *Rationing in Ireland meant shoppers in places like Dublin's Moore Street hunted eagerly for bargains.*
Photo: G. A. Duncan

3: German Spies and the IRA

A t the time of the Second World War, large numbers of Irish nationalists saw Hitler simply as someone who revised unfair boundaries and defended his people's rights. Accordingly, they were inclined to see a lot of the accounts of German violence as nothing but British propaganda. It was barely a generation since the War of Independence, and memories of the brutalities of the Black and Tans were still fresh in many people's minds. This attitude is reflected in a comment which the noted republican Dan Breen made to the Free State's only Jewish TD, Robert Briscoe: 'The Germans and the Italians are not the people that murdered and robbed my people for 700 years'.

With the outbreak of the Second World War, the Irish Republican Army (IRA) went to work again on the old principle that 'Britain's difficulty is Ireland's opportunity', and began a bombing campaign in British cities. At home, they started the Emergency period with a flourish, breaking into an Irish army depot at the Magazine Fort in Phoenix Park, Dublin, in December 1939. They made off with ammunition supplies for their armoury of Thompson sub-machine guns. In all, they got away with thirteen lorries packed with most of the army's reserve supply of ammunition. However, the bulk of this was recovered in a series of raids, and shortly afterwards the Emergency Powers Act was passed, which included measures that could be used against the IRA.

The government cracked down mercilessly on IRA activity, and interned up to 1,100 of its members during the course of the War. In addition, several IRA activists were executed — Paddy McGrath and Thomas Harte in 1940, Richard Goss in 1941, George Plant and Maurice O'Neill in 1942 and Charlie Kerins in 1944. No publicity was permitted about these executions, and any public agitation for mercy was ignored. The executions were mainly carried out by the Irish army, but O'Neill and Kerins were hanged by the British hangman, who was brought over specially for the purpose.

The conditions in which IRA prisoners were held were punitive. Prisoners in Portlaoise went 'on the blanket', refusing to wear prison clothes; they were kept in solitary confinement and were permitted neither letters nor visitors. Again, there was no publicity about the situation. Sean McCaughey, who had been C/O of the Northern Command of the IRA, went on hunger-strike in protest, and died after twenty-five days; the government would not relent.

Above: Colonel Dan Bryan, head of the intelligence services that combated both the IRA and German agents.
Courtesy Military Archives

By the end of the war, in the Free State, six policemen had been shot and six IRA men executed for their deaths; three IRA men had died on hunger-strike;

Opposite page (top): Hitler in the role of stern leader.

three had been shot by detectives; one had been shot by his own comrades, accused of being a spy. IRA activities had included several bank raids; but the organisation was largely leaderless and uncoordinated during this time. It was also split by rivalries and suspicion. By the end of the war, the IRA had no Chief of Staff or Army Council, and was effectively dormant.

An IRA campaign also continued in the North, and was met with equal ruthlessness from the authorities there. In 1942, six IRA volunteers were sentenced to death there for shooting a policeman and de Valera appealed to Churchill for clemency. He also encouraged a strong campaign for reprieve in the United States. In the end, all but one man were reprieved — Thomas Williams was executed in September 1942.

Above: Máirtín Ó Cadhain's book was begun during his internment as a Republican during the War. This famous novel marked a renewal in Gaelic writing, which created a modern literature in the native language.
Drawing by Charles Lamb R.H.A.

De Valera's concern in this regard contrasted with his treatment of IRA men in his own jurisdiction. He had also appealed for mercy for two IRA volunteers sentenced to death in England for involvement in an IRA bombing of Coventry which had killed five people. He wrote to Chamberlain, 'The reprieve of these men would be regarded as an act of generosity, a thousand times more valuable to Britain than anything that can possibly be gained by their death'. Both men were executed in February 1940; Chamberlain regretted the necessity, but could see no alternative.

Germany was alert to the possibility of infiltrating Ireland and using it as a base for espionage, but G2 was equally alert to this. As a matter of course, all the overseas legations in Ireland were closely watched, and their phones tapped. In all, only about a dozen agents managed to enter Ireland from Germany, and these encountered little success.

Edouard Hempel, the German envoy in Ireland, had warned the SS against any idea of using the IRA. In his view, it was useful for Germany that Ireland was neutral, and it would be a pity to lose this advantage:

> England would be given a pretext for intervening — which she would probably welcome — and Irish neutrality as well as the possibility of a future utilisation of the Irish cause for our interests would be prematurely destroyed.

Anyway, Hempel was convinced that the IRA would be of little use in espionage. One of the few successful German spies, Herman Goertz, agreed with this assessment, saying, 'In spite of the fine qualities of individual IRA men, as a body I considered them worthless'.

Goertz, who arrived in Ireland in May 1940, evaded arrest for nineteen months, but achieved very little with his time. An attempt to sail IRA messengers over to Germany failed when the

Left: Police photos of Herman Goertz.
Courtesy Military Archives

Above: Goertz's funeral after his suicide — a last flutter of the Swastika. The funeral was attended by the IRA.
Photo: Gerhard Stalling Verlag

IRA volunteers could not agree on which of them would command the boat. Goertz found IRA members better at talking than doing:

> When Stephen Hayes [Chief of Staff] boasted to me on one occasion that he had 5,000 sworn members ... I told him that I would be entirely content with 500 if these 500 understood how to obey an order.

Goertz spent some time imprisoned in Athlone and in Arbour Hill, and after the War wished to remain in Ireland. However, the Allies demanded the extradition of German internees, and Goertz was arrested again. He was given parole to wind up his affairs, but took poison before he could be deported, and died in Mercer's Hospital. He is buried in Deansgrange cemetery, Dublin.

Despite the unlikelihood of an invasion of Ireland, German planes frequently overflew the Irish coast, photographing possible landing places (a series of these pictures was published in Berlin in 1942). In early 1940, extremely secret meetings had taken place in London between G2 and members of the British forces, to discuss cooperation in the event of a German invasion which, it was felt, could possibly be effected by parachute. This was called the 'W Plan'. It was agreed that British forces in Northern Ireland could cross the border to help defend the Free State, and various strategies were discussed. The Irish Army was provided with extra equipment from across the border. In December 1942, two British officers travelled to Ireland and were escorted by General McKenna of the Irish Army on a tour of ports and harbours. However, by 1943 it was clear that an invasion of Ireland would not serve the purposes of either side in the war.

Right: Everyone in the country was issued with a gas mask for use in the event of an air raid. Courtesy Drogheda Museum

4: Censorship

In order for Ireland to maintain a stance of neutrality during the Second World War a system of severe censorship had to be put in place. Not only could the State not be seen to take sides in the War, but public discussion of the combatants or any of the events of the battlefield could not be permitted. In addition, all media — newspapers, radio, cinema — had to be rigorously controlled and monitored.

Ireland was already used to censorship following the Censorship of Films Act of 1923, and the Censorship of Publications Act of 1929, and there seems to have been little resistance to the idea. The Controller of Censorship was responsible to Frank Aiken, first Minister for Defence and later Minister for Coordination of Defensive Measures. The Controller also worked with Colonel Liam Archer, head of G2, and the press censor, Frank Gallagher.

In May 1939, the Department of Justice issued warrants to G2 to authorise the implementation of a secret postal censorship system which was to run alongside the existing 'open' system. These operations were run from a building on Exchequer Street, in Dublin. Staff was limited (about 200 people), so only about 10 per cent of mail to Britain and Northern Ireland was censored.

Above: Private letter, opened and resealed by postal censor.

Mail from public figures who were known to have connections with the Axis powers was a target for the censors, and it seems that G2 even intercepted some diplomatic cable traffic. Phone calls from legations in Dublin — both Axis and Allied — were listened to from a room at the top of the GPO and telegraph and wireless transmissions were also censored. There was not much resistance to the censorship of private mail; people understood the need to prevent espionage. Apparently the letters of Catholic clergy were never opened; however, a Bishop's Lenten pastoral was censored, when it expressed a hope that Britain would win the War. Censorship was employed in order to safeguard the national interest and its task involved not only the prevention of information seepage (details of weather included in football match reports, for example) but also the collection of information from the post.

The Press

The authorities were not inclined to interfere too much with the newspapers, for fear that they would close down completely. They preferred to influence the emphasis of a report rather than eliminate the facts from it. This was simply censorship, rather than direct control over every word that was printed. It was intended to be subtle, but large areas of blank space in the middle of a page

Opposite page (top): Cartoon depicting Bertie Smyllie, Editor of The Irish Times *during the Emergency period.*

tended to give the game away. Newspapers became very careful about what they covered but tried hard to defend their rights of free speech. Hector Legge, for example, editor of the *Sunday Independent*, had many clashes with Frank Aiken. The censor would suppress any material that was likely to be a threat to public order, or that was obviously biased in one direction or another (attacks on communism were, however, permitted). On one occasion, Chief Censor Michael Knightly complained to Eason's about posters advertising British newspapers which:

seem to take it for granted that we in Ireland are participating as belligerents in the war with Germany and thus give offence to our own people. An example of the latter type was provided last Sunday with the *Sunday Chronicle* with a poster bearing the slogan: 'HOW HITLER HOPES TO WIN US OUT'. Note the 'US', which could not have failed to give offence to a great many people here....

Above: Nazi book-burning spree — real censorship beside which the Irish literary censorship paled.

Of course, one of the main risks to Ireland's neutrality was the large number of British newspapers which were sold throughout the country every day. Consequently, if an issue of one of these contained an article that overstepped the mark, it would be removed from circulation. *The Daily Mirror* was banned in 1940, and publications such as *Cavalcade* and the *News Chronicle* were banned from time to time. English papers had had a huge circulation in the Free State, but as supplies of newsprint dwindled and transport was disrupted because of limited supplies of petrol, many of the British publishers ceased sending papers to Ireland. Oddly enough, Catholic missionary magazines were often banned as well, for example if they described attacks on missionaries overseas by such countries as Japan. Sixty missionaries were murdered in Manila, for instance, and in 1945 four Maynooth missionaries were burnt to death. Such stories were immediately censored, even though the US envoy David Gray protested vigorously.

One of the most aggressive editors in defence of the public's right to know was Bertie Smyllie, editor of *The Irish Times*, which had always had a pro-British slant. Smyllie believed that the newspapers should be left to censor themselves and

THE NATIONAL PRESS
16 SOUTH FREDERICK ST.,
DUBLIN,

Will publish on the 3rd Dec., 1941,

"An béal boċt"

An entirely new work in Irish
by
MYLES NA gCOPALEEN.

An exhaustive and illuminating treatise on the Gaeltacht district of Corkadorky, with cover and a map by
SEAN O'SULLIVAN, R.H.A.

An céad leabar agus an leabar is fearr ar Saeltact Corca Dorca.

Price 3/6, by post 3/9.

Limited First Edition. Order Now.

Above: Despite censorship, Irish writing in both English and Gaelic throve during the War — the heyday of Myles na gCopaleen and Patrick Kavanagh.

Aiken's alterations were an exercise in nit-picking which caused him a good deal of grief. He seems to have enjoyed the constant battle of wits, though he strongly resented the view that there was nothing to choose between both sides in the war. As he wrote to the Assistant Controller:

> I still believe that the people of this country have a right to free thought. I believe that it is part of my job to encourage them in the exercise of that right. Evidently, it is your job to stop me, and you have the power.

Another recalcitrant editor was Sean O'Faolain, whose journal, *The Bell*, began production in 1940. It contained literary prose, poetry and topical articles, and was often in trouble over its opinion pieces.

In Ireland, overseas news had always been received from foreign news agencies, mainly the British organisations — Reuters

Above: Sean
O'Faolain, editor of
The Bell. *Perhaps
the leading literary
figure of the period.*

and the Press Association — though there were also American sources, such as Associated Press and United Press. Ireland was reliant on these agencies for foreign news rather than on overseas correspondents. Other neutral countries were not so restricted. Switzerland, for example, had independent correspondents operating from abroad, and did not see 'moral neutrality' as desirable anyway; they allowed their newspapers to express their own points of view. The Irish authorities refused to provide any moral framework for the war; all belligerents were of equal value, and their activities were to be equally ignored. The use of the word 'Nazi' was banned. Those British newspapers who wanted to sell in Ireland had to bow to the Censorship Board, and the Board occasionally put pressure on British correspondents based in Ireland to publish articles giving a sympathetic hearing to Ireland's neutrality.

Although Frank Aiken knew of the atrocities of the Nazi concentration camps long before the end of the War, and further atrocities committed by Japan, all publication of such stories was forbidden. When censorship was lifted at the end of the War, the country was flooded with news of the camps, accompanied by grisly photographs, but even then many people were found to say that it was all British propaganda, and that the pictures were posed deliberately.

Right: Articles from
The Irish Times *as
marked for removal
by the censor's
office.*
*Courtesy Charles Orr
Archive*

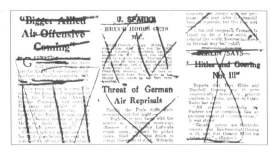

Above: The Gate Theatre combined an enthusiasm for Gaelic with the presentation of advanced modern plays from abroad.

As well as newspapers, radio, films and theatre were also censored; it is said that Bing Crosby records were banned, as 'crooning' might undermine the country's moral fibre, but this may be apocryphal. Both Allied and Axis representatives were quick to notice transgressions; Edouard Hempel complained about the performance of a play called *The Refugee*, which seemed to criticise Germany. Aiken particularly interested himself in film censorship, banning, for example, Charlie Chaplin's *The Great Dictator*, which lampooned Hitler.

In all, Irish people who remember these years speak of a sense of being cocooned, protected from reality, feeling stifled. However, although Radio Éireann was strictly censored, the BBC could be listened to, even if it was not always believed (there were still strong memories of the propaganda used in the First World War, much of which was later proved untrue or exaggerated). The feeling of being cut off may also have been enhanced by the possibility that fewer people were listening to the radio during the Emergency. Figures for the numbers of radio licences issued during the period indicate a steep fall-off by the end of the War; this may have been because of a shortage of batteries to power receivers. In any event, whether for reasons of censorship or lack of equipment, reduced access to information could only have had a restricting effect on people's view of what was happening in the outside world.

In a memo to the government in early 1940, Aiken trenchantly defended the policy of strict censorship :

Above: Display in a well-stocked Dublin bookshop — a city of avid readers of political and religious works.

There are some self-styled democrats who would hold on to the peace-time liberalistic trimmings of democracy while the fundamental basis of democracy was being swept from under their feet by the foreign or domestic enemies of their democratic state....

He commended de Valera's Constitution for foreseeing the need for a government to govern by decree, in a state of emergency, and pointed out that such 'trimmings' as discussion of legislation could sometimes be dangerous to the security of the state.

Smyllie got the last word when the war ended, however. He produced a front page announcing the armistice, in which he had arranged photographs so that they formed a huge 'V' for 'Victory', a thoroughly non-neutral message which by-passed the censor completely.

The Land and its People

Above: Contemporary builder's advertisement for a modern home — the dream lifestyle of middle-class Ireland.

Above: The new generation of the country — the parents of the tumultuous 1960s.

Above: The rural economy depended on small farmers selling a few beasts at local markets.

Left: St Joseph's Mansions, Killarney Street, Dublin. Note protesting mothers even in wartime.

Right: The almost car-free streets of Cork city. Owning a car was mostly a professional prerogative.
Photo: G. A. Duncan

Below: Feeding the hens, along with butter-making, was an important part of the woman's role as breadwinner in the rural economy.

Above: Members of a men's confraternity in Limerick renew their baptismal vows — mass devotions were very much a feature of the period.

Below: A Muintir na Tire committee meets in public in Lucan, County Dublin, with both Catholic and Anglican clergy on the platform — a rare event in the period.

5: Northern Ireland

Northern Ireland, as a part of Great Britain, entered the War with it and was later to suffer the consequences at the hands of German bombers. Air raids on Northern Ireland caused widespread damage and disruption to Belfast and many people felt that the city had not been sufficiently prepared for such attacks. In general, it seems that the Northern Ireland government was not particularly competent in dealing with the problems caused by the War and it was some time before it came to grips with them. Needless to say, Northern Unionists were extremely contemptuous of the Free State's neutrality and regarded it as a nest of traitors. Already the North was suffering from a renewed IRA bombing campaign, which had started in 1939.

The Second World War meant a huge boost to Northern Ireland's industrial economy, particularly in the areas of shipbuilding and aircraft manufacture. During the war, a total of 170 ships were built and thousands repaired; aircraft parts, tanks and munitions were also produced. Harland and Wolff built and repaired ships and by 1944 employed 30,800 workers; Mackie's produced aircraft and munitions, and the Sirocco Works produced grenades and radar equipment. All of these companies were based in Belfast and also had related factories in other areas of the state. As the War progressed there was an increase in the demand for industrial workers and, for the first time in Northern Ireland, large numbers of women were employed in engineering works — from 250 in 1939 to 12,300 by 1943.

Despite the high level of employment throughout the War, morale seemed to be low in Northern Ireland and this is reflected in the productivity levels and employee behaviour of the time. During the Second World War, production output in Northern Ireland was lower than in other parts of the United Kingdom; an official estimated that the Short and Harland aircraft works was

Above: *Barefoot poverty was commonplace in the Catholic back lanes of prosperous industrialised Ulster.* Photo: UTA

Previous page (top): *Stormont Buildings.*

operating at only 65 per cent efficiency. Absenteeism was extremely high and time-keeping was generally poor. The official observed that a lot of people seemed to be doing little or nothing for their pay.

In addition, Northern Irish industry suffered from a considerable amount of industrial unrest during the War. From 1940, strikes had been declared illegal, but there were 270 strikes in the course of the Second World War in Northern Ireland, mainly for the purpose of obtaining better wages and conditions. The importance of Northern Ireland's role in Britain's war effort seemed to encourage management and unions to use it as a bargaining chip. In 1944, five shop stewards were imprisoned after a one-month aircraft and shipyard strike, and this almost caused a general strike two months before D-Day, until a wage rise was agreed.

Low morale seemed to affect mobilisation as well as industry, and only relatively small numbers from Northern Ireland volunteered for the armed forces. For a time there even seemed to be an unofficial policy of refusing outdoor relief to unemployed single men, possibly in an attempt to make them join the army, but this was short-lived.

In 1939, at the start of the War, it was suggested that conscription be introduced and the Stormont government was keen to push this idea forward, anxious to be seen to be doing its bit. However, a very strong campaign against conscription was waged and, in the end, it was not applied to Northern Ireland at all. Some of the strongest opposition came from the United States, which felt it might upset the Canadians if they thought that conscription could also be imposed on them. The Free State opposed the idea for the sake of the nationalist population in Northern Ireland. There was always the risk that many nationalists might refuse to be conscripted, and that the IRA might decide to defend them. The North would lose more than it would gain if such a situation came about. The Stormont government was extremely angry that conscription was not extended to the province, feeling that it made Ulster look unpatriotic.

The Bombing of Belfast

Northern Ireland's war defences were utterly inadequate, and little effort was made to prepare the public for what lay ahead. In September 1940, light balloon barrages were set up over the cities of Belfast and Derry, and one RAF squadron was transferred from Edinburgh, though its fighters were only fully operative in daylight. No searchlights were in use until early 1941, despite warnings of the risk of air raids, nor was there any provision

Left: The Falls Road, the centre of Catholic Belfast, in peacetime.

made for a smokescreen. It was obvious that Belfast could be a particular target for bombers because of the shipyards and other heavy industry situated there. However, there were only seven operational anti-aircraft batteries to protect the entire city and air-raid shelters were available for only about one-quarter of the population. Although the city had 10,000 ARP (Air Raid Precautions) volunteers, they were without proper training or equipment.

As with the defence of the city, the emergency facilities were less than adequate. The Belfast mortuaries could hold only 200 bodies in all, and there was provision for emergency housing for only 10,000 people. In fact, at the beginning of the Second World War Belfast was the most unprotected and least prepared city in the United Kingdom. In the early stages of the War there was an assumption that it was too far for German bombers to come, but after the fall of France this was no longer the case.

Northern Ireland experienced the terror of German bombs in 1941, on the nights of 7–8 April, 15–16 April, 4–5 May and 5–6 May. A total of ten hours of bombing ravaged the city, leaving about 1,100 dead and 56,000 houses (53 per cent of the total number in the city at the time) damaged or destroyed. Around 100,000 people were made temporarily homeless, and the cost of the damage was estimated at about £20 million. The official figure for deaths in

Right: Belfast after the blitz — fire brigades from the south came to the city's aid.

April was 745 (the actual number of fatalities was probably nearer 900), with 430 seriously injured. A mass funeral was held for the victims on 21 April. The total of casualties for May was only 191, as so many people had left the city by that time.

The civil defence forces were overwhelmed by the devastation, and help was sought from Britain and the Free State. The air raids caused huge damage to Northern Ireland's industrial capability and as much as 45 per cent of its shipbuilding capacity was lost. Aircraft production was interrupted for the best part of a year. Telephone cables were knocked out, dislocating the communications of the RAF and the anti-aircraft batteries, and ending any effective defence.

De Valera immediately agreed to send fire-brigade services north, to help the overstretched services there. This compromised strict neutrality, but stronger emotions were at work. He

*Left:
Bombed
heart of
Belfast.*

*Will the Right Hon. member come with me to the hills and to Divis
mountain? Will he go to the barns and sheughs throughout Northern
Ireland to see the people of Belfast, some of them lying on damp
ground? Will he come to Hannahstown and the Falls Road? The
Catholics and Protestants are going up there mixed and they are talking to one another. They are sleeping in the same sheugh, below the
same tree or in the same barn. They all say the same thing, that the
government is no good.*

TOMMY HENDERSON, MP, STORMONT, 13 MAY 1941

> *Seldom have we seen such a sight. Huge shipbuilding sheds and docks are already burning. Hit at the beginning of the attack, some of them are already burnt out and have collapsed, still smouldering. But nearby, enormous fires are developing from the patterns of bursting incendiary bombs. We drop our bombs of both light and medium calibre alongside the existing fires. We are simply creating new ones as do the other aircraft. Soon, while we circle the target, a sea of flame opens up there below us. In the middle of all this, we see bombs of the heaviest calibre crashing into storehouses, docks and shipyards, ripping them apart. Gasometers explode and fuel tanks are torn open with enormous flashes reaching upwards. Burning ships are lying in the Victoria and Musgrave Channels. One explosion follows another. Incendiaries, detonations and bursting flak shells. Dazzling tracer trails and blazing fires. All surpassing each other and interacting in a brilliant spectacle.*
>
> FRITZ KRAUSE, GERMAN WAR CORRESPONDENT
> OVER BELFAST, 4–5 MAY

was criticised in some quarters at home for this decision, because at that stage of the War Germany was looking victorious, and would be unsympathetic to such help. It is possible that the later German bombing of North Strand in Dublin was not accidental, but was meant as revenge for this act of neighbourliness and to warn the Free State of the risks of becoming involved with the Allies. Fire brigades arrived in Belfast from Dublin, Drogheda, Dundalk and Dún Laoghaire.

By the end of May 220,000 people had fled from Belfast not to return

Above: Sir Basil Brooke, the Prime Minister of Northern Ireland.

[Experiences of ARP volunteer in Belfast]

What they had to do was work in pairs. Two men would drag a corpse out of the morgue and into the back yard. One, using an old-fashioned cutthroat razor, would cut or loosen the corpse's clothes, while the other would search pockets for identification, money, and valuables. These, if found, were placed in a small canvas bag which was tied around the corpse's neck. If the corpse was fouled by excrement, the clothes were cut off. The corpse was then lifted and placed in a coffin and, if stripped, covered with a shroud. The head, unless mutilated, was left exposed. A lid was placed over the coffin but not nailed down. The coffin was then carried to the outer yard to be shipped to the central hall downtown, where casualties would be exhibited for identification.

BRIAN MOORE, *THE EMPEROR OF ICE-CREAM*,
ANDRE DEUTSCH, 1966

until the bombing had stopped. As many as 10,000 people crossed into the Free State for shelter. Of those who stayed in the city, thousands left it each night to shelter in the countryside. The Stormont government considered this to be defeatism, and appealed to people to return, but it was a practice common to every major British city that suffered air raids. Derry was not bombed at all, even though it was a vital naval base, and also the location of a school of anti-submarine warfare. Joe Walshe, of the Irish Department of Foreign Affairs, is said to have convinced Edouard Hempel that Derry's only industry was shirt-making, and that it should be spared.

A fruit of the nightly exodus from Belfast was the coming together of the Catholic and Protestant communities which had previously been separated from each other. During this time the breaking down of a few barriers did occur, though the effects were not long-lasting. Another important result was the revelation of the shocking poverty and ill-health of Belfast tenement dwellers, who were billeted in rural areas. Promises were made to improve welfare services, and this began after the war, following Britain's example. A ministry of health and local government was established in 1944, and in 1945 a Housing Act created the Northern Ireland Housing Trust.

Above: *Guarding the coast of Northern Ireland, as seen by official war artist Robert Scanlan.*

Soon after the Belfast air raids three fighter squadrons were allocated to Northern Ireland and a huge programme of shelter construction was begun. A billeting and evacuation scheme was also designed, and the creation of a national fire service agreed. A 'home guard' was established which was a volunteer wing of the B-Specials. In 1940, 26,000 people enrolled in the new organisation, and it was used to help maintain internal security and to assist in the protection of military installations. Both the Home Guard and the new fire service required an oath of allegiance to the state, and this discouraged Catholics from joining either of them.

People united in criticising the Stormont government, which was revealed as hidebound and incompetent. It had apparently given parliamentary time to discussing how best to protect the Stormont buildings and the huge statue of Edward Carson, rather than concentrating on how to provide air-raid shelters for its citizens. It had also made the momentous decision to have all dangerous animals in Belfast Zoo shot, in case they escaped. Both unionists and nationalists could see that there was no consideration for the ordinary population, and that no forward planning had taken place at all. There was initial loyalist suspicion that nationalists had been sending secret signals to Germany, or attracting the bombers by shining lights, but it was soon clear that both communities had suffered equally from the devastating attacks, largely in the working-class areas around the docklands.

The Northern Ireland prime minister, James Andrews, refused to listen to criticism or to reshuffle his government. However, he was startled by the loss of a safe unionist seat in a Belfast by-election, to a candidate of the NI Labour Party. Unrest

Above: The arrival of American troops in Northern Ireland — their arrival marked the real turning point of the War. Drawing by official war artist Edward Ardizzone.

continued; there was a wave of strikes in 1942, which delayed urgent war work and shocked Churchill, but still nothing changed. Following a rebellion by back-benchers and junior ministers, Andrews was finally forced to resign, and Basil Brooke (later Lord Brookeborough) became prime minister, promising to rejuvenate the government. It took him some time to impose his authority on the 'old guard', as he was seen by some as too liberal.

High British war-time taxation helped to generate a huge tax surplus in Northern Ireland and this formed part of the North's Imperial contribution to the Treasury. In the end, this amounted to £131 million over the War years, as opposed to £29 million between 1921 and 1939. Many in Northern Ireland felt that this should entitle them to greater decision-making powers, but such matters as rationing, prices and the allocation of raw materials were controlled from London throughout the War.

> *Coming in with a Yank on a jeep*
> *All the girls in Derry thinks its cheap.*
> *With their clothes up to their bums*
> *And their chewing Yankee gum,*
> *Coming in with a Yank on a jeep.*

The Americans Arrive

A defining moment for Northern Ireland's participation in the War was the arrival of American troops in the province in January 1942. De Valera used this as an opportunity to bring up the partition question again:

> ...no matter what troops occupy the six counties, the Irish people's claim for the union of the whole of the national territory and for supreme jurisdiction over it will remain unabated.

The Americans were annoyed at being seen as an 'army of occupation', but de Valera felt that for him to accept the US arrival

There is an elaborate formula for getting chewing-gum. First you go to a sweet-shop, and they say they have had no gum since before the war. They say they wish they had gum now, because it's caught on great.

After that you find an American soldier, and this is the hard part, because you have to arouse the interest of the American soldier by saying: 'What's cookin', good-lookin'?'

This arouses his interest, and now you say: 'What's buzzin', cousin?' to set him thinking.

After he's thinking, you strike right home, putting it as clearly as possible. You say: 'Got any chum, gum?' Let me get that exactly right. You say: 'Got any gum, chum?'

I trailed a tall, olive-green American Air Force lieutenant down Dawson Street. ... I stopped by the kerb, saying rapidly under my breath: 'Got any gum, chum, got any gum, chum, got any gum, chum?'

The lieutenant came abreast of me. I stopped him. I said: 'I do hope you don't mind my speaking to you like this, and you're probably rushing off to get a train. Americans are always in such a hurry [mad laughter]; but could you possibly spare me a little chewing-gum. I've given up smoking, and my nerves are running up and down the handle-bars of my bicycle.'

The lieutenant looked pained, as these polite people do at the discovery of suffering. 'Gaash,' he said, 'that's baad, but baad. Look I gaat no gum by me, but my chum, Lootenant Taamas, in the Hibernian Hotel, he's gaat a stack. You call him up. My name's Snyder. Be glad to help out. That's real tough about those nerves of yours.'

...In the end I walked out with a packet of Juicy Fruit, a packet of Beech-Nut, the box of assorted candy drops, and a small cylindrical packet of lozenges called 'Life-Savers — Five Flavors, Mixed Fruit Flavors.'

My mouth now feels as if a tiny old lady wearing lavender-scented slippers had trailed her knitting, dipped in raspberry cordial, right through it.

PATRICK CAMPBELL
'AN IRISHMAN'S DIARY', 20 AUGUST 1945

Above: US troops receive a warm welcome in rural Ulster. Drawing by Bryan de Grineau. Picture: *Illustrated London News* Picture Library

without any protest would be seen as an acceptance of partition. He was extremely annoyed, in his turn, that he had not been consulted in advance. There had been anti-Irish protests in the United States over Ireland's neutrality, and for a while many people in the Free State feared that the Americans might invade from the North in an attempt to force Ireland into the war. President Roosevelt had to assure de Valera that America 'had not the slightest thought or intention of invading the territory or threatening Irish security'. Indeed, the Americans were seen by many others as a guarantee that Britain would not now invade.

By May 1942, there were 37,000 US troops in Northern Ireland, and a year later, preparing for the Normandy invasion, there were 120,000. At one point there were 149 American ships based in Derry, with 20,000 sailors: Derry was the most important escort base in the north-western approaches. As in Britain, the American soldiers were highly popular with local women, and with children, to whom they provided sweets and cinema shows. Such an infusion of aliens into an already divided community occasionally caused friction; in Antrim town in 1942 a black American was killed in a fight between US troops and local men.

Relations with the Free State

One problem for the Northern Ireland government during the War years was the IRA, which had begun a new bombing campaign in Britain in 1939, causing 127 explosions and killing six people. This campaign did not last, but the arrival of US troops in the North caused the organisation to renew its efforts to end partition. RUC officers were attacked, and two were killed. Six IRA volunteers were arrested and sentenced to death, but only one, Thomas Williams, was executed, in September 1942. Further attacks took place on the RUC and B-Specials, but the government moved to round up IRA suspects, and over 300 were interned. A curfew was imposed in the Falls Road, Belfast, and the IRA became quiescent again. Efforts in Northern Ireland to curtail IRA activity were greatly helped by de Valera's unrelenting campaign against the organisation in the Free State.

Just as the Free State's neutrality leant towards Britain rather than away from it, so too did it lean towards Northern Ireland. For example, a secret cross-border electricity connection was set up in case Belfast was bombed and its electricity sources disabled. Northern Ireland's large industries were booming because of wartime orders, and it would be devastating if electricity supplies were lost. No publicity surrounded this decision, and no enabling legislation was passed by either jurisdiction. The fact that the connection would compromise Free State neutrality never seems to have been mentioned.

The Stormont cabinet was deeply suspicious of any links with the Free State, but finally agreed the connection in May 1941. This timing was bad for the Free State Electricity Supply Board, which was suffering from a scarcity of coal (coal rationing began later, in 1942). It would be very embarrassing for the ESB to be supplying current to Northern Ireland while running short for their

Above: *War meant short periods of hectic action, followed by long periods of inaction, the latter recorded here by official war artist Robert Scanlan.*

own customers in the Free State. It was agreed that if the Belfast power station had to be shut down, its coal supplies would be transferred across the border. The connection was finalised in January 1942, and the electricity link remained until 1947, when it was allowed to lapse.

Another important piece of cross-border cooperation was the Erne Scheme — a major plan to use the Erne river as an electricity generator — which was first proposed in 1942. It would involve work in Northern Ireland to control the release of water from the Erne lakes, for which the ESB would cover the costs. Some of the electricity generated would be sold back to the North. Again, Stormont was very suspicious of cooperation of this kind, but flooding in the area was a perennial problem, and the scheme would involve a massive land drainage programme which would be of great advantage to local farmers. Dublin approved the scheme in August 1943, but the principle was not accepted in Northern Ireland until 1946 — there were fears that electricity supplies could be blocked by the Free State if the North became dependent on them. The huge scheme was finally completed in 1957, and is still in operation.

At the end of the War, all workers in Northern Ireland were given two days' holiday with pay. U-boats near the coast were ordered to surface and make their way to Derry, and 28 U-boats were later scuttled near Rockall. Northern Ireland's economy, given a boost by wartime conditions, settled into a period of prosperity and relative peace. A large programme of post-war reconstruction got under way, including slum clearance and improved health services, and the state also benefited from the British education improvements, enlarging access to education through a 1947 Act. Britain, of course, underwrote much of the cost of these improvements.

The Call to Arms

Right: General Costello (far left) and his staff.

Below: Citizens in arms — an initial unit drawn up in Christchurch Place, Dublin. Courtesy Military Archives

Above: *Soldiers of the 26th (Old IRA) Battalion on the move.*
Photo: G.A. Duncan

Below: *The call-up included men of all ages, some with experience in the Troubles.* Photo: G. A. Duncan

Above: Irish Army artillery unit in action

Below: Machine-gun unit under camouflage.
Courtesy Private Collection, Richard Hanley, Military Archives

Above: *An anti-aircraft unit with gun and rangefinder (foreground).*
Courtesy Military Archives

Above: *An Irish Air Corps plane, actually recycled from a downed British Hawker Hurricane.* Courtesy Military Archives

Below: *Troops on manoeuvre crossing the Blackwater — men were drowned in this operation.* Courtesy Military Archives

Below: The Taoiseach inspects the honour guard during the 25th anniversary of 1916. Interestingly his title, under the 1937 Constitution, had the same meaning as *Führer* and *Il Duce*.

6: In Uniform at Home and Abroad

The Army

In 1939, the numbers in the Irish army stood at 7,600 — under-strength in many respects, and particularly so in light of the impending war. By late 1940, however, following government appeals, the ranks had swollen to 37,000, and this figure had risen to 40,535 by the end of 1942. The wartime recruits were known as 'Emergency men' or 'Durationists', since their service was only temporary.

Although the army had strengthened in numbers, it remained ill-equipped and there were severe shortages of guns, ammunition and anti-aircraft equipment. The Cavalry Corps, however, did acquire several armoured cars; these had been made in Ireland using motor-car chassis.

Both Britain and the USA restricted the supply of weapons to the Free State, in part because they did not want the army to be able to defend the Treaty ports. Britain did accept orders from Ireland for various weapons before the War, but without giving precise delivery dates; the outbreak of War caused any such orders to be sidelined. In an attempt to procure arms, General Michael Costello was sent to the United States. However, it was illegal for the US War Department to supply weapons directly, and ammunition costs were prohibitive. In the end General Costello did succeed in acquiring 20,000 Springfield rifles, but levels of equipment and ammunition remained poor.

Pay and conditions in the Irish Army could not compare with those in its British counterpart, and at least 7,000 Irish soldiers deserted to the Allied forces during the War years, earning 22 shillings per week as opposed to 18 shillings at home. To any army the loss of a trained soldier is serious, and one of the responsibilities of the Irish intelligence service was to trace deserters and, if possible, arrest them. Most units in the army remained below

In the early days we performed arms drill with wooden rifles, but early in 1941 William Filgate of Lisrenny Hall, one of our platoon leaders, made a gift to the platoon of sixty Brown Bess flintlock muskets, two brass flintlock blunderbusses and one nine-foot blunderbuss, together with a supply of powder and ball...They had been issued to the 11th Militia about 1798.

Our platoon now conducted army drills with the Brown Bess. We also fired the muskets, using the black powder and ball...On pulling the trigger, there was a loud click as the cock holding the flint struck the pan cover, then (usually) the powder in the pan would flash, followed by detonation of the main charge in the barrel, and the ball and a dense cloud of smoke would emanate from the muzzle. There was a memorable recoil...

Finally our long-awaited Springfield rifles were issued, each with forty rounds of ammunition, and enabling us to exercise with the regular army.

REMINISCENCES OF FRANK MATTHEWS, COUNTY LOUTH LDF
IRISH SWORD, EMERGENCY ISSUE, VOL. XIX 75/76, 1993–4

Right: The D-Day landing — the Allies begin the conquest of Europe in July 1944.

Page 81: Prepared to meet the invader.

strength for the duration of the War and each year 30 per cent of applicants were rejected, mainly for medical reasons. There were also many exemptions for agricultural leave or compassionate leave, and individuals to whom these applied were placed on reserve.

A memo from the General Staff to the Taoiseach, Eamon de Valera, in December 1940, emphasised the need for a strong army, while admitting that it could never defend the country against a serious attack. The memo continued:

> On the other hand, it is believed the plan outlined in this memo will enable a prolonged resistance to be put up, and as a result time will be gained and a measure of world sympathy obtained. By achieving this we at least establish our right to unity and independence on the conclusion of world peace.

Since the Free State was neutral, all the Irish Army could do was remain in a state of preparedness for invasion, whether by

Britain or Germany, or by the United States, as some expected. The army was also engaged in anti-IRA activity, preventing the cutting of phone wires and so on. In addition, it took part in 'civic' duties such as turf-collecting, and had a Construction Corps — designed for unmarried unemployed men — that was involved in road-building, drainage works, and aerodrome improvements.

The army occasionally ran up against the civil service, in the shape of the Department of Local Government; the army wanted the Department's technical and road staffs to act as volunteers with the engineering corps. It was also inclined to remove road signs and so on without the proper authority. In addition, the army mined bridges without considering the effects on water pipes, sewerage and electricity lines which ran alongside. Arguments of this kind were not settled until mid-1942.

The army intelligence service, G2, involved in counter-espionage, became dominant during the War over the Garda Síochána intelligence service, G3. This was particularly the case with regard to external relations, and G3 concentrated mainly on anti-IRA activity. Relations between the two services occasionally became strained, but overall they worked well together. There was also a Supplementary Intelligence Service, a network of people chosen to help army intelligence, particularly in the south of the country,

Left: Camped on the Blackwater — the Irish army in action

near the Treaty ports. These people, mostly one-time republicans, were to remain in place if the country was invaded, and operate a counter-intelligence service. They were not officially employed, and were paid only expenses. It was this group that foiled Herman Goertz's planned escape from Kerry in 1941. At the end of the War, they were not eligible for the official defence forces' 1940–1945 Emergency service medal, and medals were issued secretly to them in 1951.

Auxiliary Services

The Local Security Force (LSF) was set up in 1940 to act in the area of civil defence. It operated under the control of the Garda Síochána though its leaders were elected by the membership itself. Erskine Childers, secretary in the Local Government department, was emphatic on the importance of such a force:

> Each cottage, each village, each town must be a fortress in itself. If we were attacked, twenty armed men in some remote parish who could delay the passage of troops might well prove to be a turning-point in our defence.

The LSF was later split, and part of it became the Local Defence Force, which acted as an army reserve. Initially, the LDF was organised by the Garda Síochána, but responsibility for it was transferred to the army in 1941. The LSF had 44,870 members by the end of June, 1940, and by the following October this figure had risen to 145,306. The LDF was never such a large organisation, and its membership reached the total of 10,000 at its highest.

Groups such as the Irish Red Cross (established in 1939), the St John's Ambulance Brigade and the Knights of Malta readied themselves for civil defence duties. Volunteers were needed for auxiliary fire services, casualty clearance and evacuations, but there were grave doubts about whether resources were adequate or training effective. An assessment of ARP personnel in Belfast had concluded that part-time volunteers were of no real value in such a capacity.

The Irish Navy came into being through a clause in the Hague Convention, which demands that a neutral country must control its ports if it's to remain neutral in time of war.... The call went out, therefore, to Irish yachtsmen, and any others accustomed to the sea, to take over from the storm-tossed infantry, who were openly protesting that an extra 2s 6d a day danger-money was no compensation for being so far out of their element.

The call, at least in the case of the Dublin Port Control Service, produced a varied bag, of about thirty men. There was a hard core of part-time dockers and longshoremen from the North Wall, with a sprinkling of cynical youths from the seaside town of Dún Laoghaire, who'd joined in the belief that even this lash-up couldn't be as bad as the Army. There was also myself, the only Protestant among the whole elite corps — an unavoidable disability that caused me for four years to be regarded, philosophically, by my shipmates, as an enemy agent.

PATRICK CAMPBELL, 'SEAN TAR JOINS UP',
COME HERE TILL I TELL YOU,
HUTCHINSON & CO., 1960

Below: *A senior officer inspects the Local Defence Force unit at Clongowes Wood College, an elite private school.*

In early 1940, the Red Cross set up an Emergency Hospitals' Supplies Depot in Dublin, and provided services for refugees, housing over 700 people for some weeks after the Belfast bombings. In late 1944, as the War drew to a close, arrangements were made to set up an Irish Red Cross hospital in Saint Lô, Normandy. This was established in August, 1945 and provided medical services to a shattered community until the end of 1946.

Above: Marine Serviceman on duty. Courtesy Military Archives

Marine Services

Below: The Irish Navy on patrol. Courtesy Military Archives

The Free State navy was still in the early stages of development, having only two ex-fisheries vessels, *Murchú* and *Fort Rannoch,* each armed with a 12-pound gun, two machine-guns and some depth-charges. (The *Murchú*, a former British gunboat, had shelled Dublin during the 1916 Easter Rising.) There were also three motor torpedo boats in service. As Captain T. McKenna said of his own experiences, 'We were on our own with nothing but a vintage Fishery Protector armed with a three-pounder and solid shot, to look after 5,127 square miles of the territorial sea on a perimeter of 783 miles and a coastline of 1,970 miles'.

Left: Oscar Traynor, the Minister of Defence, presents a prize shield to an Army officer.

Ireland was obliged to set up a Marine Service because of the Hague Convention, which required neutrals to patrol their own coastal waters in order to examine passing shipping and also to clear mines. The rather motley service that was put together in the Free State consisted mainly of officers and ratings with a background in the Royal Navy, some men from the Merchant Navy, and a number of fishermen and yachtsmen. There were also men from the Department of Agriculture fishery protection service, though these individuals retained their civilian pay and employment conditions. The Marine Service was largely disbanded at the end of the War, but it had laid the foundations of Ireland's present-day naval service.

Irish ports should have been mined for protection, but Britain refused to sell any mines to the Free State. Instead, Thompson's Foundry in Carlow improvised a type of mine that was then filled with explosives by the Ordnance Corps. These devices were used to mine the harbours of Cork and Waterford. Britain had constructed a huge mine barrage across St George's Channel, and many of these came adrift and floated to the Irish coasts. Any that were found by the shore were detonated by the Marine Service. One of the first magnetic mines that was seen outside Germany was washed up on an Irish beach, and it was immediately sent over to the British for examination.

The Irish Coastguard had been scrapped in 1923, but with the onset of the Second World War the presence of a coastwatching body was essential. Accordingly, a new service was established in early 1939 and lookout points were put into operation around the country at 88 different locations. Initially, the lookouts were posted in tents, but they were soon provided with concrete huts. Each volunteer lookout team consisted of about eight men led by a corporal, and the volunteers were required to live within six miles of their posts. They worked in shifts of eight to twelve hours and, as their main function was to observe, they were unarmed.

Accusations were frequently made by the Allies that German U-boats were refuelling in Irish ports (despite the country's desperate lack of fuel). While this was untrue, it is possible that U-boats occasionally used isolated west-coast bays for shelter.

Air Corps

The Irish Air Corps was completely under equipped for fighting during the Second World War. At the time, the only army officer who seemed to appreciate the importance of air power for the future was General Costello who, with Aiken's permission, tried to acquire some American aircraft in 1940. His efforts were opposed by the army Chief of Staff and the Officer Commanding the Air Corps, who insisted instead on trying to acquire planes

> ...It was sticking out a mile that if he [Hitler] came into England and conquered England that Ireland would be next ... he had only to send a platoon of girl guides to take Ireland because we had a tiny army at the time, utterly dependent on England for their cast-offs in the way of arms and things and not really capable of defending anything. I mean I thought I should do something about it.
>
> JOHN JERMYN, IRISH VOLUNTEER IN BRITISH ARMY,
> FROM *VOLUNTEERS ORAL ARCHIVE*, UCC

from the British. In the event, they got neither. At the start of the War, the Air Corps had some sixty planes of one kind or another. It did acquire some British planes during the War, either by purchase, or by agreement of salvage after a crash-landing. None of these planes ever suffered a mechanical failure, because of the skills of the Air Corps mechanics. Fuel shortages were a severe constraint on activities.

The Air Corps recorded violations of Ireland's air space, and liaised with Allied air units in Northern Ireland on such matters as recovery of crashed planes, but overall its functions were extremely limited.

Above: Ray Collins, who won a Distinguished Flying Cross. An RAF officer born in Cork, he was killed aged 26 on active service in the summer of 1942.

At the end of the Second World War, two Emergency medals were issued, one for the defence forces (including the chaplaincy and the Army Nursing Service) and one for the volunteer services.

The Irish Abroad

It is difficult to ascertain fully how many Irish men and women (including Northern Ireland citizens) joined the British services during the Second World War; estimates range from 50,000 to 120,000 to 165,000. Dominions Office figures for Irish in the services, in 1944, were given as 27,840 from the Free State, and 26,579 from Northern Ireland, based on place of birth. The Royal Navy and the Royal Air Force had about 10,000 Irish personnel each. Many who enlisted gave English addresses on joining, or had been living in Britain when war broke out, so the lists do not necessarily reflect the reality of the situation.

Those who did join the British Army had various reasons for doing so. Some came from Anglo-Irish families, and were following a family tradition of soldiering, while others simply despised Hitler, or wanted to earn a living, or wanted the excitement, or were perhaps trying to evade the police, or responsibilities at home. As one Irish serviceman said, 'I knew Hitler was a baddie, but essentially it was a job ... If I could have got a job in Dunmanway, I would have stayed there'. Many found themselves wondering what they would do if Britain tried to take back the Treaty ports by force, and they were ordered to invade their homeland; at some stages of the war, this looked like a distinct possibility.

> *...[He] suddenly got up, rushed the post and hurled two grenades at it. When he ascertained that some, but not all, of the enemy had been killed he returned to his section, seized a Bren gun, and again dashed forward to within thirty metres of the post and with accurate fire completely silenced it. He then went forward again, through heavy rifle fire, and successfully rescued his section leader who had been wounded in the shoulder.*
>
> ACCOUNT OF THE EXPLOITS OF RICHARD KELLIHER, WHO WON A VC
> IN NEW GUINEA, FIGHTING THE JAPANESE

The Irish who served in the British Army during the War inhabited a sort of no-man's-land in Ireland. There was confusion over whether they needed travel documents to travel home on leave, but it was finally agreed that service leave documents could act as travel permits. On grounds of neutrality, Irish members of the British forces could not wear their uniforms if they were visiting their homes in the Free State, and civilian clothes were provided at Holyhead for them to change into before travelling across the Irish Sea. The Department of External Affairs found itself dealing with enquiries about Irish personnel missing in action, and passed most of these on to the Red Cross. The severe censorship of the time meant that reports on emigration and enlistment were banned.

> *We went right in under high clay cliffs, just like the ones behind Killiney station, and beached the craft. Machine gunfire was rattling against the sides of the vessel, and we had to lower the bow doors down by hand. They stopped halfway. I was officer in charge of the doors, desperately heaving on the winch. Then I discovered we had lowered the doors onto an anti-invasion tripod, with a Teller mine on the top. We should have been blown apart. We backed away very, very carefully.*
>
> NAVAL LT MICHAEL D'ALTON [NORMANDY SURVIVOR],
> *THE IRISH TIMES*, 6 JUNE 1984

Above: Lieutenant Colonel Jack O'Riordan, who fought the Italians in West Africa and the Germans at the battle of El Alamein.

After the War, strenuous efforts were made to write such Irish volunteers out of Irish history. A British Legion Remembrance Day parade was banned in 1945, although permission was given for a parade in 1946. The government probably did not want much public expression of exactly how many Irish people did fight in the War, which might seem to discredit the policy of neutrality. In fact, many of the Irish in the British forces did feel that Ireland was right to be neutral, as a small, undefended state, but equally they felt that they themselves had a duty to fight fascism. Most of the veterans seem to have colluded in the post-war silence, and were reluctant to participate in ceremonies held on Remembrance Day. Church services were often picketed by republicans on that day of commemoration, and British Legion poppy-sellers were harassed.

In all, Irish fighters had won eight Victoria Crosses and 780 military decorations in the Second World War, but their sacrifices were covered over, like some kind of shameful secret, for most of the next fifty years.

Below: Mopping up German resistance at El Alamein. Many in the Irish army at home, including General Costello, had relatives who fought in the Western Desert. British official photograph

7: Ireland and the Holocaust

The problem of how the Free State was to deal with refugees, particularly Jewish refugees, arose early in the Second World War. At the time, the Jewish community in Ireland did not have a chief rabbi and its affairs were handled by the Jewish Representative Council. Through this body the greater community fought hard and despairingly to have some of their co-religionists permitted to land in Ireland, in order to save their lives.

De Valera was very sympathetic to these pleas, but other arms of government, such as the Department of Finance, were less willing to listen. It was explained to petitioners that Ireland already had an unemployment problem, and that letting in 250 Jewish refugees — an early proposal — would make this problem even worse. Sean Lemass thought it would be more practical to offer concrete help, such as sending food supplies to Europe, rather than allowing hundreds of refugees into the country. At the same time, the Department of Justice kept to a very conservative interpretation of the Aliens Act of 1935, that is, to allow in as few aliens as possible. Since Jewish refugees lost the citizenship of whatever state they had come from, many countries feared that they stay forever if they allowed them to enter during the War. Even aliens with valid work permits would become refugees when the permits ran out.

There were groups in Ireland who fought for the admission of Jewish refugees, such as the Society of Friends' Committee for Refugees and Aliens, and the Jewish Refugee Aid Committee of Éire. The Church of Ireland and the Catholic Church also helped to secure refuge in Ireland for European Jews, but the efforts of both Churches were more usually concentrated on assisting Christian refugees. In 1938 a group was launched specifically to support the cause of Christian European refugees, mainly from central Europe:

> Let us now show that we, too, can be generous and prove to the world that the Irish people believe that Christians of whatever race or blood are sons of the same Father Whose brotherhood is shown, above all, in this, that they love one another.

In the meantime, the 1916 Veterans' Association had passed a motion:

> That we hereby register our emphatic protest against the growing menace of alien immigration, and urge on the Government the necessity of more drastic restrictions in this connection.

Statistics indicate that in 1939 there were 2,354 aliens in the Free State, with the largest group being apparently 1,143 Americans. Civil servants felt that an increase in the number of aliens, particularly Jews, would lead to problems of prejudice and possibly to physical violence. In 1938, the assistant secretary of the Department of Justice said:

> There is a feeling in this country ... that there are [sic] an undue number of Jews resident here, and that any increase in the present number might easily lead to a definite anti-Semitic agitation arising.

Opposite page (top): Terenure's modern synagogue was built after the War. Unlike in many parts of Europe, the small Jewish community in Ireland had not been decimated by the War.

Above: Robert Briscoe, a leading figure in the Irish Jewish community, later Lord Mayor of Dublin.
Photo: G. A. Duncan

Minister Patrick Ruttledge wrote much the same thing to Robert Briscoe, the Jewish Fianna Fáil TD, later in that year:

... there are anti-Jewish groups in the country who would only be too glad to get an excuse to start an anti-Jewish campaign and those groups could get no better slogan than that the native Irish worker was being ousted by cheap imported labour.... The conclusion I am inclined to draw is that the existing Jewish community in this country would be well advised in its own interests not to encourage Jewish immigration...

Anti-Semitism

In Dublin, particularly, there was a strong vein of anti-Semitism, and such groups as the People's National Party advocated the blacklisting and public insulting of Jews. Its leader, George Griffin, fulminated:

An Taoiseach's father [de Valera] was a Portuguese Jew. Erskine Childers' grandmother was a Jewess. Mr Ruttledge has Jewish connections by marriage — and 'Jew' was written all over the face of Mr Sean Lemass! Practically all the Fianna Fáil TDs are in the clutches of the Jews!

This party had broken away from the Irish Friends of Germany, another pro-German and anti-Semitic group, who seemed to have links with the IRA, but which had dissolved by mid-1941. The People's National Party managed to print an anti-Semitic newspaper, called *Penapa,* in late 1940, but produced only two issues before it was banned. It is possible that they may have got funding from the German or Italian legations. There were also clandestine radio broadcasts disseminating anti-Semitic propaganda, and the Italian envoy had to be summoned by the Department of External Affairs to explain some anti-Semitic bulletins issued by his legation.

In response to these manifestations, a group of people including Frank Duff (later founder of the Legion of Mary) and Leon Ó Broin, then a Department of Finance official, established the Pillar of Fire Society, to facilitate Christian-Jewish dialogue at regular meetings. However, it met only three times, and folded apparently because of restrictions which the Catholic Archbishop of Dublin, Dr John Charles McQuaid, wished to impose, such as having Christian lecturers only.

By autumn 1942, Colonel Dan Bryan, as head of G2, was well informed about the extent and horror of the Holocaust, and de Valera soon received a telegram appeal from Isaac Herzog, Chief Rabbi in Palestine, confirming that a huge tragedy was in train:

... Deportations from Germany Holland Belgium France Norway to Polish ghettoes thence centres mass executions continue unabated.... May our heavenly father vouchsafe you his counsel and guidance and make you providential agent for salvation millions innocent men women children facing imminent threat of annihilation.

Above: Dr John Charles McQuaid, Archbishop of Dublin, who had strict ideas on inter-faith matters.

Above: Anti-Semitism in Germany lay at the root of the final solution.

The director of the Agudas Israel World Organisation, Harry Goodman, proposed that the Department of External Affairs should issue 100 visas to selected families, and give discretion to its envoys in Europe to issue visas for those who were in most urgent need of an opportunity to emigrate. Herzog sent another telegram in July 1943:

> Horrified by report some 80,000 Jews in Italy native and refugees threatened with deportation to Poland which means certain death....

The secretary of the Department of External Affairs contacted his envoy in Italy, but was reassured that its racial laws were about to be repealed — this did not, of course, happen.

Opposite page: The proprietor of Polikoff was a refugee from Europe who had established his clothes firm in the safety of the Irish Free State.

Over a number of months, Ireland received lists of names of people who were seeking visas. The country was apparently prepared in principle to accept 500 Jewish children (the Irish Red Cross section dealing with this decided to cross out the word 'Jewish' when they were making the matter public). None arrived. Strong attempts were also made to rescue over 200 Jewish families who were stranded at Vittel, in Vichy France, but the Germans ultimately refused permission for them to go, and many were sent instead to Auschwitz. Irish diplomatic missions continued to make appeals on behalf of Jews in death camps, but to little avail.

No one knows how many Jews were allowed into Ireland during the War; it may have been about sixty. Robert Briscoe was later rumoured to have run a kind of 'underground railway', but there is no evidence to support this.

Below: During the Nazi era 6,000,000 Jews and other minorities were killed.

8: Workers at Home and Abroad

A t the time of the Second World War, the trades union movement in Ireland comprised about 150,000 members. However, there was a split between those unions that were strictly Irish and those which had affiliations to the British TUC. In addition, among the nationalist unions, there was a deep rivalry between the Irish Transport and General Workers' Union and the later group founded by James Larkin, the Workers' Union of Ireland.

Within the Irish TUC, which was led by William O'Brien of the ITGWU, there was a strong movement to expel the part-British unions or at least limit their activity, and the Fianna Fáil government favoured this course of action. To have British-based unions operating in the Free State could seem to be a compromise of strict neutrality; some people even feared that Britain might use them to sabotage the Irish economy.

The government saw the outbreak of war as an opportunity to introduce powerful industrial relations legislation, reducing the powers of unions to strike:

Above: Demolition workers prepare to rebuild the country.

Above: Jim Larkin, charismatic trades union leader.
Courtesy ITGWU

Account must be taken of the protective and social services which the community at great cost has provided for industrial and commercial workers. The country is, therefore, entitled to take steps to prevent the loss and inconvenience inflicted upon the community by a major strike in any essential industry....

This concern was heightened when over 2,000 Dublin Corporation workers went on strike in early 1940. They were demanding a wage increase of 8 shillings per week but the Corporation was allowed to offer them only 2 shillings. Government pressure eventually forced a return to work.

The new legislation, which was passed in 1941 and was strongly influenced by the ITGWU, introduced a system of negotiating licences. This meant that a union could not operate within the Free State unless it had deposited a sum of money — between £1,000 and £10,000 — with the High Court. Essentially, this would force the smaller, poorer unions to amalgamate or dissolve, and would also possibly eliminate the Workers' Union of Ireland, the ITGWU's main rival. Another requirement was the establishment of a tribunal, which would decide which union was the official representative of specific groups of workers. This was designed to limit the activities of the British-based unions. (In 1946 the tribunal was held to be unconstitutional and discriminatory.)

Under the Emergency Powers Act, the government introduced a Wages Standstill Order in 1941, which effectively froze wages for the duration of the war. It also removed legal immunity for any industrial action that was taken in contravention of the order. This created an outcry, and Larkin organised a huge demonstration in protest. The subsequent campaign for repeal of this order drew little support, and was weakened by the ongoing conflict between O'Brien and Larkin. Lemass later offered some increases under the Order, but only to unions who had registered themselves under the 1941 Act.

The War, of course, was having a severe effect on the cost of living. By 1944, the cost-of-living index had risen 70 per cent above its pre-war figure, but average wages had risen by only 30 per cent at most.

When Lemass returned to the Department of Industry and Commerce in 1941, he introduced a new Trades Union Act that he hoped would conciliate union leaders. This removed some of the clauses they had objected to in the earlier Act. The government preferred to have union cooperation. Besides, a general election was due, and the Labour Party had been making inroads on government support, winning 15.7 per cent of the vote in the 1943 general election. This raised the party's total of Dáil seats from nine to seventeen. James Larkin was re-admitted as a member of the Labour Party, and chosen as a candidate, but the ITGWU instantly demanded his expulsion. When Labour refused, the IGTWU disaffiliated from it in January 1944, and five Labour TDs seceded to form the National Labour Party, claiming communist infiltration had taken place within Labour. As a result of this split, in the 1944 election, the Labour vote dropped to 8.8 per cent, giving them only eight seats, while National Labour took four seats. The Labour Party had seemed for a moment to be in a position to challenge Fine Gael as the main opposition party, but the rift between it and the ITGWU had scuppered these hopes.

Above: *William O'Brien, trade union leader, often opposed to Larkin.*
Courtesy ITGWU

The Workers' Union of Ireland finally affiliated with the Irish TUC, and ten unions, including the ITGWU, immediately disaffiliated and formed the Congress of Irish Unions. This split weakened the union movement as a whole. It also worried the government, who had found it easier to deal with one grouping. In 1946, Lemass introduced an Industrial Relations Bill which set up the Labour Court, on which workers and employers had equal representation. Under its auspices, the first National Wage Agreement was formulated in 1948.

In the public service, problems were caused by the steep rises in the cost of living consequent on the War. The Emergency Powers Order (No. 38) of 1941 had stabilised pay, but the cost-of-living index was 120, up by 35 points from the level at which pay had been frozen. Legal proceedings were brought, and it was ruled that the Minister of Finance had acted within his rights. A mass meeting took place in January 1942, uniting the civil service unions, and small concessions were eventually won, of about one shilling in the pound. Subsequently, Emergency bonuses were paid to public servants.

Left: The Emergency provided women with new opportunities for work in industry — here in a clothing factory.

Right: Bringing milk to the local co-op, the origins of today's great agribusiness enterprises.

Working Abroad

One reason for the levels of apathy in the union movement in Ireland, and the lack of a vigorous response to wage levels, was the disappearance of large numbers of workers to Britain, to work in the manpower-starved industries there. Up to 190,000 Irish workers are believed to have gone to England during the War years, an annual average of about 34,000. However, the statistics are not very reliable as they are based on the number of travel permits issued; people could hold more than one permit, and many may not have used the ones they held at all. In 1939, remittances from England to Ireland were worth over £1 million, and by 1941 this had risen to £2 million; the amount kept on rising.

At the start of the War, the British government launched a campaign to recruit Irish workers. The Irish government wanted only unemployed workers to leave and essential workers, such as those involved in food production, were restricted from going to Britain. Those with experience of agriculture or turf-cutting were also discouraged from emigrating.

Irish workers in Britain had to have travel permits and to have a job arranged before leaving Ireland. They were described as 'conditionally landed', which meant they could not be conscripted until two years had elapsed since their arrival. Because of the IRA campaign in Britain, which led to a Prevention of Violence Bill in 1939, Irish immigrants had to register with the police, and report any changes of job. They were mainly employed in the armaments and aerodrome construction industries in the large industrial cities.

Above: *Aer Lingus flight crew herald the beginning of a new era (with actor Godfrey Quigley on the right).*

Dublin had a large reservoir of unskilled and semi-skilled workers, and 20 per cent of those leaving Ireland came from there. The largest number of emigrants left between 1941 and 1943, but security restrictions leading up to the invasion of Normandy meant a sharp fall-off in 1944, when access to Britain was closed off. At this point, the number of men leaving Ireland had risen to just over two-and-a-half times that of women. However, by 1946 the difference between the numbers of male and female emigrants had become more or less balanced again. Most of the work available in Britain for women was factory work and domestic service, and many rural women saw such employment as a chance to leave a life of domestic drudgery and limited autonomy. Besides, wages in Britain were noticeably higher than at home, rising by 20 per cent between 1941 and 1945. During the War, the difference between British and Irish wages rose from 16 per cent to 32 per cent for males, and from 8 per cent to 31 per cent for females.

Above: The 1940s saw the arrival of film-making by young radicals as an instrument of social and political action.

The government itself could not be seen to be aiding emigrants for fear of seeming to endorse emigration, and thus admitting that the Free State could not support its own people. However, numerous voluntary bodies did offer assistance to those who left Ireland. Archbishop McQuaid established an emigrant section in the Catholic Social Welfare Bureau in 1942, which was mainly concerned with their moral welfare. However, it also helped emigrants with practical and social problems, and efforts were made to prevent isolation.

Such high levels of emigration meant that Irish unemployment rates dropped from 15 per cent in 1939 to 10 per cent in 1945. Towards the end of the war, the government feared that a mass return of workers would completely destabilise the Irish economy, causing unrest and riot, but this did not transpire. Many workers did not return at all, and those that did were absorbed into the expanding industrial economy of the Free State. Those who stayed in Britain could hold on to their social insurance funds, which they would have lost by leaving. There was a huge demand for labour in Britain after the War — for reconstruction and the building of the new Welfare State — and Irish workers needed little persuasion to stay.

9: The Impact of War

Transport

Despite its neutrality, Ireland was not exempt from the effects of the Second World War, and people's routines and everyday needs became more affected as rationing and petrol shortages began to bite. The availability of fuel became a major problem and public transport almost ground to a halt. There was a small revival of horse-drawn traffic, but bicycles were the most common form of transport. Some cars ran on gas from large gas bags on the roof.

Despite the restrictions, Dublin gained something of a reputation for being a good place to visit for British servicemen on leave. Foods such as meat and dairy products were freely available, and the entertainment aspect of the city remained lively. Large numbers of racehorses, along with their retinues, had arrived from Britain early in the War, and race-meetings were well attended. Other sports also flourished, but, of course, without international fixtures.

Getting to Ireland, however, was more of a problem, as services such as the mailboat were affected by the general disruption of the war and also by fuel shortages. Within the country itself

Left: Even with war-time rationing men's clothes advanced an image of style and fashion that was aspired to rather than achieved by many Irishmen.

QUALITY

IN the Men's Department—as well as every other department in Todd's—QUALITY is the keynote. In these days of coupons it is the most important consideration — for you must surrender the same amount of coupons whether you buy good quality or not.

ODD, BURNS & CO. LTD. MARY STREET, DUBLIN

Previous page (top): *Bargain cabbages.*
Photo: G. A. Duncan

limited coal supplies meant a gradual deterioration of all rail services; Dublin and Belfast grew further apart. (There was, however, a thriving cross-border smuggling trade.) A Transport Act in 1944 amalgamated Great Southern Railways and the Dublin United Tramway Company into Córas Iompair Éireann (CIE), a national transport company. It was some time before this could operate efficiently, because of the fuel shortages. Meanwhile, the canals came into their own again, and twenty-nine new barges were ordered in 1942 to help in the transportation of turf.

The air link with Britain was kept open, and flights left Baldonnel daily for Liverpool and London. They carried mainly business travellers, and cattle buyers coming over from Britain. In 1940, Collinstown airport was officially opened in County Dublin, but it closed each day at 5.30 p.m. Also in that year, Aer Lingus acquired its first DC3 aircraft, but found difficulty in getting spare parts. In 1942, a Dublin–Shannon service was inaugurated for a brief time. However, in 1944 as the Normandy invasion drew nearer (D-Day), air traffic stopped completely from

April until September. The approach of D-Day also resulted in telephone contact with Britain being cut off, for reasons of security.

A study of the traffic through Dublin Port at the beginning of the War would reveal the extent to which the Free State was dependent on foreign shipping. The government established Irish Shipping in 1941, and had managed to acquire ten ships by the end of that year. The Custom House docks and the port area were provided with air-raid shelters, and Alexandra Quay was used for the storage of coal and turf reserves. As in the case of air travel, sailings were restricted between April 1944 and June 1945 because of the Normandy invasion.

> To anyone privileged to leave the warlike atmosphere of England and visit Ireland, which is enjoying a state of peace, it seems as if one has moved into an unreal world. To the traveller arriving from England's black-out, Dublin's sea of lights is like a magic lantern. The tempting delicatessen in the shop windows and above all the peaceful routine and the enjoyment of leisurely gossip remind the visitor of long forgotten times.
>
> REPORT IN *NEUE ZÜRCHER ZEITUNG*
> AUGUST 1942 (SWITZERLAND)

Right: Imports and exports, even through small Irish ports, were important to the Irish economy.

The Arts and Media

Newsprint shortages meant that newspaper pages grew smaller and smaller and resulted in a corresponding increase in the price per copy. English newspapers, which had had a wide circulation in the Free State, gradually withdrew from the market, because of costs and difficulties in distribution. The Irish newspapers that remained were so heavily censored that few actual items of news were published. For Irish people it was as though they were living within a glass jar during the Second World War — they were only partially aware of events that were occurring outside the country.

Culturally, Ireland's isolation was seen by some as an ideal opportunity to revive the Irish language. Both the army and the volunteer services had Irish-speaking units, and there was a movement to simplify the spelling of Irish to make it more accessible.

A KINGSTON SHIRT MAKES ALL THE DIFFERENCE

Above: 'Going to the pictures' was the most popular form of entertainment during the Emergency period — here satirised by Alan Warner in a cartoon for a Dublin clothing firm.

Some modern currents began to move during these years. The White Stag Group, consisting of a number of displaced artists from Europe who moved to Ireland, allied with modern Irish painters and established an Irish Exhibition of Living Art in 1943.

Another modern current that began to emerge was expressed by the foundation of the Irish Housewives' Association in 1942. This association voiced concerns about social issues, and rejected the idea of the 'idealised housewife'; they were interested in practical ideas about improving women's lot and fought for such advancements as rural electrification.

Above: The dancing stage at Carna Fair, a painting by Richard King, typifying the traditional life admired by de Valera — this represented what he wanted to protect by maintaining Ireland's neutrality.

Opposite page (top): Iveagh House, gifted to the government in 1939, from which the policy of Irish neutrality was directed and defended.

Opposite page (bottom): Flower seller in the centre of Dublin, a city at peace.

First page this section: A British view of quaint war-time Dublin, a drawing by John Betjeman's friend, Osbert Lancaster, of the birthplace of poet Tom Moore, in Aungier Street.

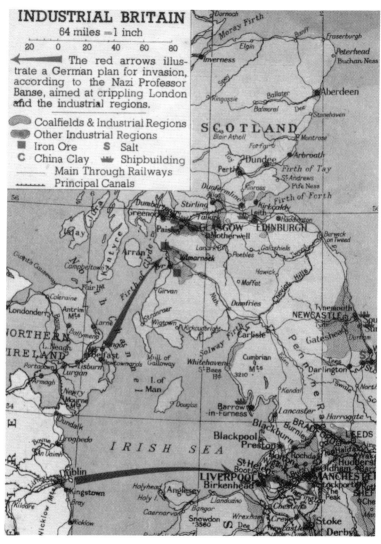

INDUSTRIAL BRITAIN

64 miles = 1 inch

20 0 20 40 60 80

◄━━━━ The red arrows illustrate a German plan for invasion, according to the Nazi Professor Banse, aimed at crippling London and the industrial regions.

Coalfields & Industrial Regions
Other Industrial Regions
■ Iron Ore   **S** Salt
C China Clay   ⚓ Shipbuilding
─── Main Through Railways
······ Principal Canals

Above: Contemporary map of possible invasion routes from a German-controlled Ireland into the industrial heartlands of Britain in the Midlands and Clydeside, prepared by Nazi academic Professor Banse.

Above: The uniforms of a
nation in arms, painted by
Tom Nisbet for Call to Arms.

Right: The flag of the Local
Defence Force volunteers.

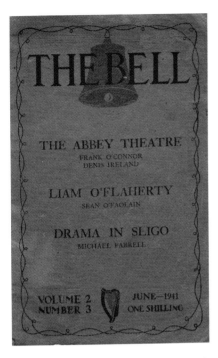

Above: Device of the National Planning Conference, echoing many socialist symbols of the period.

Top left: The Bell, a popular and vigorous liberal magazine edited by Sean O'Faolain, in which many of the best Irish writers of the period appeared.

Bright colours for brighter days! Dubarry proudly presents this gay and carefree wedge-heeled model which interprets their hopes for to-morrow. Fashioned in tan calf and mustard suede, with green calf wedge and beading. Its colours strike a bright and happy note. Supplies to-day are limited, but remember if you are disappointed a happy tomorrow may not be very far away.

DUBARRY SHOEMAKERS LTD.

FOOTWEAR MANUFACTURERS   BALLINASLOE, EIRE

Left: After the War, Irish industry attempted to produce new and attractive lines for export, in this case stylish shoes.

Opposite page: A handbook of post-war planning, issued in connection with the National Planning Conference in Dublin.

1/3

LEABHAR NA hEIREANN 1942

RECONSTRUCTION NUMBER

IRISH YEAR BOOK

Above: Irish art of the period: Kinsale *by Paul Henry, an illustration for Sean O'Faolain's* Irish Journey *(1940).*

Left: Fish and Chips, *a view of Belfast by surrealist Colin Middleton.*
Courtesy of Irish Museum of Modern Art

'What I love about your Dublin,' said the foreign visitor, 'is the heavenly smell of peat.'

'Pete who?' I said, twisting another newspaper into strips and poking it into the fire, lying flat on my face, with my eyes running.

'Peat,' said the visitor, 'the stuff you're lighting.'

I blew madly into the fire, until the room began to swirl around. 'It's not called peat,' I said, 'it's called turf.'

The foreign visitor thought for a moment, and then he said, 'But how do you light it?'

I gave one final blast, and threw the bellows into the fire.

'You take four bundles of sticks,' I said, 'and dry them in the gas-oven until crisp. While the sticks are drying you dry a quarter of a ton of turf, piece by piece, over an electric stove. Set the fire and touch a match to it, and then start rushing up and down the back stairs, carrying up more and more turf, and flinging it on the fire, until it's time to go to bed.'

The foreign visitor looked uncomfortable, and then he said: 'I suppose, actually, you're probably joking.'

PATRICK CAMPBELL, 'AN IRISHMAN'S DIARY'
THE IRISH TIMES, 14 FEBRUARY 1946

Right:
Shortages affected all housewives — even those who self-consciously shopped through the medium of Gaelic.

Ní miste beit ag bráit ar béantúisí

CLOVER

Maiṙbeoil Ḋeiṙce Leasaiċe,
Sciaġanna Ḋeiṙce, baġún,
Ġamaí, Sáisíní aġus Pocóġa,
aġus rl.
Crúbána "ERINOX" aġus
Ġréiḃín ḃlasca "CLOVO"
Iaṙṙ iad san uile.

Above: The modern age reaches rural Ireland — a modernist shop front by Michael Scott for Williams's of Tullamore.

As well as political censorship, literary censorship was tight; the work of author Kate O'Brien was banned, as was the publication of *The Tailor and Ansty*, by Eric Cross, which reproduced the sometimes bawdy conversation of a West Cork tailor and his wife. Theatre censorship was less severe. A play by Robert Collis, *Marrowbone Lane*, produced in the Gate Theatre, created a good deal of interest in the housing conditions of the Dublin poor. This later led to the Marrowbone Lane Fund, created to feed starving Dublin children.

Ernest Blythe, director of the Abbey Theatre, appealed for £200,000 in 1941 in order to establish a national film industry, but without success. The government did fund several documentary films during the Emergency period, though these were made by an American company and were intended to explain the Irish neutrality policy.

Two Irish comics, Jimmy O'Dea and Harry O'Donovan, took regular parts in a BBC Home and Forces programme called 'Irish Half-Hour', which was aimed at the large number of Irish troops in the Allied forces. BBC Northern Ireland was keen to use more Irish performers for this audience, but such a policy was implacably opposed by the Regional Director, Douglas Marshall, who was unionist in sympathy.

Domestic Supplies

Food rationing was severe at times, and the lack of wheat meant that bread got gradually coarser and blacker. It was made illegal to serve wheaten food twice at one meal in restaurants and cafés. Plans were made for communal kitchens, where cooked food could be supplied to the public, but these were never put into operation. By 1943, the Free State was receiving only a fraction of its requirements of imported commodities: 25 per cent of tea, 20 per cent of petrol, about 15 per cent of paraffin and gas coal and 22 per cent of textiles; no coal was available for domestic use at all. (Sean Lemass was christened 'half-ounce Lemass' because of the tea ration.) Gas rationing was strictly policed, and an official known as 'The Glimmer Man' could appear at your door without warning to check whether you were using gas outside regulation hours. Food restrictions hit poor families worst, as bread was a staple of their diet. The middle classes supported a thriving black market where tea could be had for £1 (20 shillings) a pound, instead of the 3 shillings it should cost. The shortage of cigarettes was a severe deprivation.

Coal was one of the most essential supplies for Ireland, and during the 'Phoney War' the Free State stockpiled it furiously, eventually accumulating a record reserve of 2.7 million tons.

However, the country was still utterly dependent on the 40 million tons of coal it received annually from Britain. By June 1940, coal had already been rationed to half a ton per month per household, but in 1941 the supply from Britain was drastically reduced to 5 million tons per annum. Consequently, the domestic ration was cut to a quarter ton per month between March and October of that year. As large industry claimed more and more of the coal supplies, it became almost impossible for domestic users to get any at all. This was at a time when there was no central heating, and many people, particularly in rural areas, still used fires for cooking. Trains were seriously affected by the coal shortages, and they were kept going by supplies of 'duff', a mixture of pitch (tar residues) and coal dust. Heiton's coal suppliers produced 'Heitoids', balls of coal slack mixed with a tiny bit of turf and 25 per cent pitch, for domestic use. In March 1941, a trawler ran aground off County Wexford, and had to dump its cargo of coal overboard. All available boats salvaged the coal and dried it out; it had doubled in price in the previous year, and was well worth the effort of collecting it.

Turf became a valuable resource, and huge quantities of it were cut and stored at central points. A mountain of turf was raised in Phoenix Park, and unemployed people were deployed in rural areas to cut more. Of course, not all turf was of good quality; as one sufferer said, 'you could wring it out', and as the War went on the general standard of this fuel got worse and worse.

Left: As a part of the loosening morals of urban life, ads for lingerie became more inviting. Liquid make-up was used on legs instead of silk stockings, which were unobtainable (perfectionists painted a seam up the back of the legs).

Above: Irish industries strove to fill the gap left by the decline of imported goods — though fashions, as shown here for children, were little different from those in Britain.

Public Health

In terms of public health, the Free State did not start the Emergency years in good shape. There had been a huge rise in urban population, especially in Dublin, and the number of cases of tuberculosis, for example, had risen sharply through over-crowding and poor nutrition (deaths caused by TB increased from 1.23 per 1,000 in 1937, to 1.46 per 1,000 in 1942). It was not until after the War, in 1947 that Departments of Health and Social Welfare were established in the Free State, and proposals put in train to expand state services. This followed the Beveridge report, published in Britain in 1942, which led to the establishment of the National Health Service there.

During the War the Department of Local Government and Public Health concentrated its efforts on the prevention of infectious diseases such as diphtheria and typhoid, and Emergency Powers, No. 26 Order, 1940 gave it increased powers of detection and isolation. Public Health (Infectious Diseases) Regulations 1941 increased the number of notifiable diseases, and also the powers of medical officers.

However, this did not necessarily bring about an overnight improvement of general standards and by 1943 Britain was insisting on health inspections for Irish emigrants, because lice carried impetigo and typhus. Consequently, the Irish government instituted a health embarkation scheme to reduce national embarrassment as much as possible. Between 1943 and 1947, as many as 55,000 people were stripped, shaved and disinfected in these depots before they departed for Britain — a demoralising experience indeed.

Left: Warfare as seen by the Dublin cocktail-drinking classes — the good time to be had in war-time Dublin surprised and delighted visitors.

As tuberculosis was such a severe scourge at the time, a National Anti-Tuberculosis League was founded in 1942. However, Dr John Charles McQuaid, appointed Archbishop of Dublin in 1940, felt that such a campaign should be carried out by the Red Cross, and the League was merged with that organisation (the League had had many Protestant supporters). When Dr James Deeny joined the Department of Health, he pushed matters forward, and a White Paper was published in 1946. This subsequently led to the almost complete eradication of TB from Ireland in the years that followed the Second World War.

> *My brother arrived at my house half-dressed and shouted to me that Shannons' house was blown up. I had heard the explosions and saw the flashes and the light on the mountain. They were like flares or incendiary bombs. When I got to Shannons' Peter Breen had located Jim Shannon and I found Mick and freed him. He had been blown out of the field at the back of the house and was covered with plaster and timber and slates.*
>
> *I knew the layout of the house well so I started looking for the girls. Bridget was the first I found. She was buried underneath large stones and was dead. I worked frantically to get to Mary Ellen. She, too, was dead and had received terrible injuries. There was a huge stone lying on her head. Young Katty was also dead when I got to her.*
>
> THOMAS WARD, NEIGHBOUR, DESCRIBING THE BOMB DAMAGE AT BORRIS, COUNTY CAROW, *IRISH PRESS,* 3 JANUARY 1941

In 1944, with various schemes on the table for reorganising the health services, Dr James Deeny became chief medical officer of the Department of Local Government and Public Health. A departmental committee was set up, and produced a report which advocated the setting up of county and regional health services. The county would be responsible for family care while specialist services would be based in Dublin, Cork and Galway. District medical officers would look after about 700 to 1,000 households, and it was proposed that all services should be available to the whole population:

> The ideal to be aimed at is a national health service embracing all classes within its scope, recognising no limitation of effectiveness on mere economic grounds, and treating the people, from the health point of view, as a unit.

The department drafted a White Paper based on these recommendations and, in 1948, after several long and bitter battles and accusations of 'socialised state medicine', Ireland finally achieved the establishment of a more modern health service.

Early on in the Emergency period hospitals were asked to prepare evacuation plans; those in Dublin were to be used as clearing stations in the event of bombing, and 400 beds were to be provided outside Dublin for casualties. St Vincent's Hospital was one of those asked to provide 100 beds for air-raid casualties, and the staff were trained in the use of gas masks.

> *The shops are full of good things to eat, the streets of people who cannot afford to buy them. Light and heat are desperately short, for there is very little coal, and turf is scarce through lack of transport. The coal ration is three-eighths of a ton per two months, unless one is in a district where turf is compulsory, and that costs 64s per ton and burns badly. Doctors and Government inspectors have less petrol than the English motorist, the great country houses have their bath night once a week, bread is rationed, tea and coffee are very scarce, trains run slowly on inferior fuel, the Archbishop of Dublin has inaugurated free soup kitchens, an army is training without modern equipment, and even the Gaelic is slipping. ...And emigration — the silent indictment of a civilization which no censor can suppress — continues to threaten its human resources. This is a black picture, but it is important for the English reader to stop thinking of Ireland as an uncharitable earthly paradise.*
>
> CYRIL CONNOLLY, 'COMMENT',
> *HORIZON*, VOL V, NO 25, JANUARY 1942

The Hospital Sweepstakes fund closed for the duration of the War, since a scarcity of building materials meant that no hospitals could be built. Shortages of petrol affected doctors on their rounds, and district health nurses had to do their rounds by bike as they were forbidden to use cars. Hospitals suffered shortages of dressings and equipment, and even the nurses' veils were shortened.

The need for wartime emergency preparations yielded a long-term benefit for the country in the form of the blood transfusion scheme which was established during the Second World War. The scheme was described as having in it 'the nucleus of a national peacetime service which will be a boon alike to our patients and ourselves'. One reason for its popularity was probably the free cup of tea provided to blood donors, at a time when the tea ration had shrunk pathetically.

Dr McQuaid also was active in the area of health and provided encouragement to voluntary organisations which looked after the sick poor. He persuaded the voluntary hospitals to establish VD clinics, and expressed concern about the levels of infant mortality. The Catholic Social Service Conference was established in 1941, and the Catholic Social Welfare Bureau was founded to look after emigrant welfare.

Bombings

Ireland experienced few of the horrors of war, but there were some isolated incidents. On 26 August 1940, three women were killed when bombs fell on a creamery at Campile, County Wexford. Bombs had also fallen in the county that day at Ballynitty, Bannow and Duncormick. Those killed at Campile were Mary Ellen Kent, her sister Cathleen, and Kathleen Hurley. The explosives fell at lunch-time, when most workers had left, but two of the dead had been working in the restaurant, which was hit, and all were buried beneath debris. Several other people were injured. Nine or ten bombs were dropped in all, and they may have been intended for the nearby railway line. The plane and bombs were later identified as German, and Germany promised to pay compensation. Later that year a bomb fell in Sandycove, County Dublin, and the mail-boat was bombed as it left Dún Laoghaire harbour.

In early 1941, the Free State was again targeted by German war planes. On 2–3 January, bombs fell near Drogheda, in open country, and others landed near Oylegate, in County Wexford.

Above: The Co-Op Creamery at Campile, the first victim of German
bombs, which fell on many other places besides Dublin and Belfast.
Courtesy Military Archives

Below: Plan of the Creamery with bombers' flight paths plotted.
Courtesy Military Archives

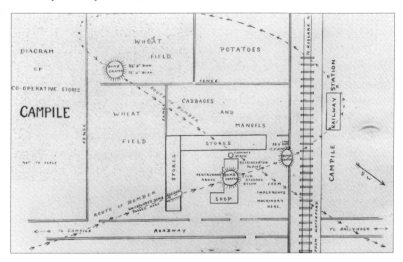

At the same time, four bombs fell on Dublin, two at Rathdown Park, Terenure, and two at the South Circular Road; about twenty people were injured as a result. A further three bombs exploded on the Curragh, County Kildare, and sea mines were dropped by parachute on County Wicklow, near Enniskerry — these did not explode and were later destroyed by army engineers. Apart from those injured in Dublin in these attacks, the only casualties occurred in County Carlow, where a farm near Borris was destroyed while the family slept. Mary Ellen, Kathleen and Bridget Shannon were killed outright, and Jim and Mick Shannon were injured. Again, protests were made to Germany.

On 31 May 1941, a large bomb fell on North Strand, in Dublin. It was the early morning, and most people were still in bed. A journalist described one body being removed on a stretcher:

> ... covered with a fine ash, though it could have been dust — everything appeared to be covered in the dust of centuries ... The body was obviously smashed beyond recognition; you couldn't even tell whether it was man, woman or child.

The final death-toll from the North Strand bomb was put at 34 or 35 people; it was difficult to be certain, because some of the remains in the City Morgue were unidentifiable. Part of a man's body was found on the railway line near Newcomen Bridge the following day. Dr McQuaid sent £500 to the Red Cross to aid the victims.

Above: The North Strand bombs and the loss of life they caused became an enduring image of the War.

Later it was said that the bombers had believed they were over Belfast, and that the British had deliberately interfered with the radar beams to cause this confusion. It is probable that British efforts were being made to stop German bombers heading to their ports, but it is unlikely that Dublin was a deliberate choice of target. In 1958, Germany paid $327,000 in compensation for this particular bombing raid.

The damage from the bombings, of course, had to be repaired and when rebuilding began, owners and local authorities were allowed to spend up to £130 without detailed approval for reimbursement. Reconstruction took a long time because so many skilled workers were in England. Dublin Corporation did not want to take on the sole responsibility for the cost of rebuilding and the owners of the wrecked houses were equally unwilling to foot the bill, even if they could afford to. Finally, under the Neutrality (War Damage to Property) Act of 1941, local authorities were given power to purchase and demolish damaged houses. Many claims, however, were not fully settled even a year after the bombs had fallen.

In June 1941, three people were killed when two houses collapsed in Bride Street, and it was surmised that they had been shaken and damaged by the Dublin bombs.

Left: The Soviet Army goes into action against fascism — the heroic allies of the 1940s would become the Red menace of the 1950s.

Planning a Post-War World

Above: Young planners at work on the National Planning Conference exhibition in 1944.

Above: Young people crowding in to see a vision of the future in Ireland, May 1944.

Above*: The City Hall to be, a more open scheme than finally evolved amid much controversy in the 1980s.*

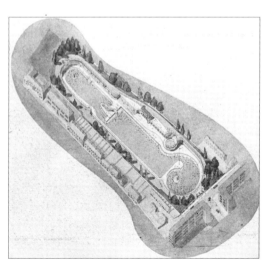

Left*: Public Baths at St James's Street, Dublin; intended as an amenity for a poor district, the baths were never built.*

Right: Michael Scott, an emerging architect of the young generation.

Below: A model of a village school — education was to become a priority.

Above: The Refined Home, *drawing by Gerald McNicholl from 1944 in the style of Osbert Lancaster.*

Right: Basil Rákóczi, the leading figure in the White Stag Group of artists in wartime Dublin, with his son. Rákóczi was one of a number of European intellectuals who sought refuge in Ireland. Courtesy Gorry Gallery

Below: New roads — the beginning of the traffic planning of today.

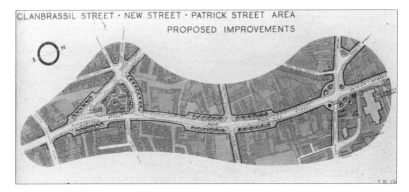

CLANBRASSIL STREET · NEW STREET · PATRICK STREET AREA
PROPOSED IMPROVEMENTS

10: Aftermath

At the end of the War, negative attitudes to Ireland's neutrality were compounded when Eamon de Valera, on hearing of the suicide of Adolf Hitler, paid an official visit of condolence to Edouard Hempel, the German legate, on 1 May 1945. To de Valera, this was the normal courtesy due on the death of a head of state — he had paid an equivalent visit to the US legation on President Roosevelt's death two weeks earlier — but it naturally appalled the victorious powers, and indeed many people within his own government. The only other neutrals who adhered to this protocol were General Salazar of Portugal and General Franco of Spain. Hempel himself, who had been greatly relieved by the news of Hitler's death, was flabbergasted. This action set the seal on an international image of Ireland — blindly neutral in its own self-interest, with no appreciation of wider considerations.

Winston Churchill, in a radio broadcast later in May, made severe criticisms of Ireland's stand. In a reply delivered three days later, de Valera gave a reasoned explanation of the background to Irish neutrality, and outlined the pressures the Free State had been under. He also praised Britain for having resisted the temptation to invade. The speech was well received in

Left: The aftermath in Europe: ruins around Köln's Catholic cathedral, a fate that Ireland escaped.

Previous page (top): New middle-class housing in Cabra. Photo: G.A. Duncan.

Ireland, and to some extent made up for the unease caused by the condolence visit earlier in the month. But Ireland's policy remained a matter for argument after the War. Fine Gael TD, Dr Tom O'Higgins, protested in the Dáil:

> We are bringing up a generation blissfully unconscious of facts ... thinking that in a world war a declaration, plus a comparatively insignificant army, is sufficient to keep a country free from war.... We have magnified our immunity from war and our neutral position into a major government achievement.

As the War drew to an end, the Allies requested neutral countries not to grant asylum to Axis war criminals. The Irish government stated that it would not grant entry to aliens whose admission would be:

> ... at variance with a policy of neutrality, or detrimental to the interests of the Irish people, or inconsistent with the desire of the Irish people to avoid injury to the interests of friendly states.

> *... [The]* Sunday Observer *of January 30th clinches the matter with a naked hammer-blow: 'Today we have to ask ourselves, can the power of the United Kingdom — can the material and financial resources of the United Kingdom — suffice to discharge all the commitments which this country has assumed or is about to assume as guarantor and defender of the world's peace?'*
>
> *Let us be as nakedly frank. This is 1944. Twenty-five years ago, in 1919 or at any time before and around it, we in Ireland would have read such confessions and perturbations with a savage satisfaction. England's difficulty was Ireland's opportunity. Our position has since altered. Some of England's difficulties are our difficulties. We are two small islands off the European mainland. We have large mutual trade and investments. Our relations are bedevilled by the historical injustice of Partition. We shall soon be within bombing range of three continents. The future difficulties of Europe, political, economic and defence, approach us both inexorably and affect us both. As free and equal and good neighbours we can be a good example and help to our neighbours in Europe in the dangers that lie ahead. Lastly, but most importantly, we have not only common difficulties but we have a common opportunity for mutual help, for our relations are more easily capable of being finally and firmly settled than those of most European states.*
>
> SEAN O'FAOLAIN, 'ONE WORLD'
> *THE BELL*, VOL VII, NO 6, MARCH 1944

This commitment was considered weak by the United States, and when it instituted the Marshall Plan in 1948, to assist in European post-war reconstruction, Ireland was not high on the agenda. Another result of neutrality was a Soviet Russian veto, for eleven years, on the entry of Ireland to the United Nations; it had not proved itself to be 'a peace-loving nation'.

Straight from the Shannon

into your home. Immense reserves of energy — enormous supplies of power. Energy and power that you can direct in the performance of your housework. Energy and power that enable you to conserve your own energy and time, to produce better housekeeping results and to reduce housekeeping costs.

USE ELECTRICITY
for every household task

Above: Electricity — together with increased industry — became more essential to Irish life in general and would affect society in unexpected ways.

Above: Machine-won turf heralded the advent of the great turf industry of later years.

Below: From field to factory — the movement in rural Ireland from a traditional to a modern economy.

Ireland ended the Second World War with industrial production down by 30 per cent, and agricultural production severely affected by a series of bad harvests. Unemployment figures stood at 62,000 men and 8,000 women, and the number of people emigrating continued to rise, reaching a total of 40,000 for the year of 1948. Rationing continued throughout the 1940s; coal supplies remained small and petrol was scarce. However, some goods remained plentiful, and supplies of bacon, dairy products, canned meats and baby foods were soon being shipped to Britain. The Red Cross also arranged for surplus blankets and cook-stoves to be sent across the Irish Sea.

Above: The Priest's Sister, *drawing of a character from* Cré na Cille, *which satirises the 'fast' young women which the war years encouraged to claim more for themselves.* Charles Lamb R.H.A.

Sweden and Switzerland — both neutral countries — made far quicker recoveries after the Second World War than Ireland; their economies were more soundly based, and their industries had been strengthened by the military expenditure of the warring nations. Ireland's industrial production managed to regain its pre-war level by 1946, and 62,000 new industrial jobs were created between 1946 and 1951. Under the control of the Department of Industry and Commerce the rate of building increased spectacularly after the War, with a particular emphasis placed on factories and roads. De Valera harboured plans to create new suburbs around Dublin in which to relocate the inhabitants of the capital's tenements, and to limit the city's population to 765,300. He also envisaged a green belt surrounding Dublin, and the growth of satellite towns in Tallaght and Malahide. Despite the extent of development plans, however, protectionism still held firm over Irish industry, and management expertise was poor. There was little effort to develop new export markets, and a period of stagnation set in during the 1950s.

Right: Desmond Fitzgerald's Dublin Airport terminal, symbol to many of the new Ireland that was emerging, fully connected to the outside modern world.

Ireland was intellectually isolated during the Emergency but, in truth, it had been so since the foundation of the Free State: many attempts at participation in international trends had been censored over the years. The country had avoided the extreme pressures of actual war, which in other countries had shaken up received ideas and hidebound administration. Consequently, in some respects, it remained unchanged; for example, the Catholic Church still maintained its primacy in the affairs of the country. In other respects, however, the War did bring about change in Ireland. The health services were developed and improved, largely due to the example from Britain, and a huge rural electrification scheme was begun in 1947, which by 1956 had connected 163,000 customers. Ireland was facing the new world with a proper Air Corps and a merchant marine service; and plans had been made to develop Shannon Airport as an intercontinental facility. The search for self-sufficiency and the dearth of fuel supplies led to the development of the Turf Board, Bord na Móna, which was highly successful in industrialising the recovery of peat for fuel.

Above: The end of the war also meant a return to such mundane tasks as cutting the grass.

The most far-reaching effect of the Second World War on Ireland was perhaps the increased sense of national identity that it engendered. The Irish Free State was initially seen as, and had felt itself to be, an adjunct to the British Common-wealth, not completely independent and autonomous. The declaration of neutrality in 1939, when its closest neighbour was about to come to grips with a massive and aggressive power, made the point once and for all that here was a new country, which was determined to stand on its own two feet. It didn't have to, in the end, and it remained dependent on British trade for several more decades, but the country's image of itself was irrevocably changed.

Left: Marshall Aid hoped to restore a continent and create a new democratic Europe — but Ireland was not included.

Bibliography

Allen, Trevor, *The Storm Passed By: Ireland and the Battle of the Atlantic 1940–41*, Dublin

Bardon, Jonathan, *A History of Ulster*, 1992, Belfast

Barton, B., *The Blitz: Belfast in the War Years*, 1989, Belfast

Bowen, Elizabeth, *The Shelbourne*, 1951, London

Butler, Hubert, 'The Invader Wore Slippers', *Escape from the Anthill*, 1985, London

Campbell, Patrick, *An Irishman's Diary*, 1951, Dublin. *Come Here Till I Tell You*, 1960, London

Carroll, J.T., *Ireland in the War Years*, 1975, Newton Abbot

Coogan, Tim Pat, *De Valera: Long Fellow, Long Shadow*, 1993, London

Cullen, L.M., *Eason & Son, A History*, 1989, Dublin

Daly, Mary, *The Buffer State: The Historical Roots of the Department of the Environment*, 1997, Dublin

Davison, R.S., 'The Belfast Blitz,' *Irish Sword* Vol. XVI, 63, 1985

Doherty, Richard, *Irish Men and Women in the Second World War*, Dublin

Duggan, M.J., *Neutral Ireland and the Third Reich*, 1985, Dublin

Dukes, Jim, 'The Emergency Services,' *Irish Sword* Vol. XIX, 75/76, 1993–4

Dungan, Myles, *Distant Drums: Irish Soldiers in Foreign Armies*, 1993, Dublin

Fanning, Ronan, *The Irish Department of Finance 1922–58*, 1978, Dublin

Farmar, Tony, *Heitons — A Managed Transition*, 1996, Dublin

Fisk, Robert, *In Time of War: Ireland, Ulster and the Price of Neutrality 1939–45*, 1983, London

Gaffney, Phyllis, *Healing Amid the Ruins: The Irish Hospital at Saint-Lo (1945–46)*, 1999, Dublin

Girvin, B. and Roberts, G. (eds), *Ireland and the Second World War: Politics, Society and Remembrance*, 2000, Dublin

Girvin, B. and Roberts, G., 'The forgotten volunteers of World War II,' 1998, *History Ireland* Vol. 6 No. 1

Gray, Tony, *The Lost Years: The Emergency in Ireland 1939–45*, 1997, London

Harkness, David, *Northern Ireland Since 1920*, 1983, Dublin

Horgan, John, *Sean Lemass, The Enigmatic Patriot*, 1997, Dublin

Irish Sword, Special Issue on the Emergency, Vol. XIX, 75/76, 1993–4

Keogh, Dermot, 'Anglo-Irish diplomatic relations and World War II,' *Irish Sword* Vol. XIX, 75–76, 1993–4

'De Valera, Hitler and the visit of condolence, May 1945,' 1997, *History Ireland*, Vol. 5 no. 3

Ireland and Europe 1919-89, 1989, Dublin

Jews in Twentieth-Century Ireland: Refugees, Anti-Semitism and the Holocaust, 1998, Cambridge

Twentieth-Century Ireland, Nation and State, 1994, Dublin

Lee, J.J., *Ireland 1912–1985: Politics and Society*, 1989, Cambridge

MacCarron, Donal, *Step Together: Ireland's Emergency Army*, Dublin

McCarthy, Charles, *Trade Unions in Ireland 1894-1960*, 1977, Dublin

Monsarrat, Nicholas, *The Cruel Sea*, 1951, London

Moore, Brian, *The Emperor of Ice-cream*, 1966, London

Myers, Kevin, 'Interviews with Normandy survivors', 6 June 1984, *The Irish Times*

Nowlan, K.B. and Williams, T.D., *Ireland in the War Years and After 1939–51*, 1969, Dublin

O Drisceoil, D., *Censorship in Ireland 1939–45: Neutrality, Politics and Society*, 1996, Cork

O'Connor, Emmet, *A Labour History of Ireland 1824–1960*, 1992, Dublin

O'Donovan, Katie, 'Were we right to stay neutral?', 3 June 1994, *The Irish Times*

O'Halpin, Eunan, 'Aspects of Intelligence,' *Irish Sword,* Vol. XIX, 75/76, 1993–4,

   Defending Ireland: The Irish State and its Enemies since 1922, 1999, Oxford

Phelan, Jim, *Ireland — Atlantic Gateway*, 1941, London

Share, Bernard, *The Emergency: Neutral Ireland 1939–45*, 1978, Dublin

Stephan, Enno, *Spies in Ireland*, 1963, London

Index